FLYING LESSONS

122 STRATEGIES TO EQUIP YOUR CHILD TO SOAR INTO LIFE WITH COMPETENCE AND CONFIDENCE

GREGG STEINBERG, PhD

THOMAS NELSON
Since 1798

NASHVILLE   DALLAS   MEXICO CITY   RIO DE JANEIRO   BEIJING

To all parents who want
to help their children
achieve greatness

Published in Nashville, TN, by Thomas Nelson. Thomas Nelson is a trademark of Thomas Nelson, Inc.

Thomas Nelson, Inc., titles may be purchased in bulk for educational, business, fundraising, or sales promotional use. For information, please e-mail SpecialMarkets@ThomasNelson.com.

Library of Congress Cataloging-in-Publication Data

Steinberg, Gregg M., 1963–
  Flying lessons : 102 strategies for equipping your child to face life with confidence and competence / Gregg Steinberg.
    p. cm.
  Includes bibliographical references.
  ISBN 13: 978-1-4016-0337-3 (pbk.)
  ISBN 10: 1-4016-0337-8 (pbk.)
  1. Emotions in children. 2. Emotional intelligence. I. Title.
  BF723.E6S74 2007
  649'.6—dc22   2007008280

Printed in the United States of America
07 08 09 10 11 RRD 5 4 3 2 1

CONTENTS

PART 4 EMOTIONAL BRAVADO: BE FEARLESS

PART 5 EMOTIONAL DRIVE: POWER ON

PART 6 EMOTIONAL BALANCE: FIND YOUR PEACE

ACKNOWLEDGMENTS

The writing of this book has been a wonderful experience and would not have come to fruition without the help of some exceptional people in my life.

I want to thank Pamela Clements at Thomas Nelson for seeing my vision and believing that I had the right stuff. I am blessed to have her as a friend, fan, and publisher. It is an honor to be associated with her and the people at Thomas Nelson, who I believe are the spiritual leaders in the field of the written word.

I also want to thank my insightful editors Jennifer Greenstein and Sara Henry at Thomas Nelson. I thank you for all the time and effort you spent on this book. You took the manuscript to the next level and made my words soar.

I also want to acknowledge all the players and parents whom I have worked with over the past fifteen years. I have learned so much from you and have tried to share many of our experiences in this book.

Last, I want to thank Beatrice J. Steinberg, who is the perfect role model for the lessons taught in this book. You instilled in me a belief that anything is possible. I am truly blessed to have been raised by a mother who cherished my vision and helped guide me down all the right paths.

MASTER YOUR EMOTIONS, MASTER YOUR WORLD

In a Native American proverb, a father tells his son about the battle that goes on inside everyone's head. The father says, "My son, the battle is between two wolves inside us all. One is weak. It is jealousy, distraction, sorrow, regret, arrogance, inferiority, fear, and self-pity. The other is strong. It is joy, love, hope, focus, kindness, compassion, confidence, and peace of mind."

The son thought about it for a minute and then asked his father, "Which wolf wins?" The father simply replied, "The one you feed."

Some parents know instinctively how to help their children feed the "strong" wolf. Earl Woods was an example. Trained by the military in both physical and mental toughness, Earl put his young son, Tiger, through what he called "finishing school." He applied some of the drills he discovered in the military on young Tiger's golf game. Earl would yell, "Out of bounds on the right!" in the middle of Tiger's backswing. Or Earl would jiggle some change in the middle of a putting stroke. Earl also gave Tiger a safety word, "Enough," which would stop the harassment. But Tiger never once used his safety word; instead he just smiled as his father tried to toughen him up. Today, many experts believe that Tiger is the most mentally gifted athlete in the world.

Unfortunately, many parents are not like Earl Woods: They lack the knowledge or skills to help their children feed the "strong" wolf. Unknowingly, they may even help to feed the "weak" wolf.

Most parents want their children to attain their potential as well as to succeed in life, but they do not know any specific strategies to achieve those goals. This book is dedicated to these parents.

Flying Lessons helps parents to harness key emotions in their children. The power of success comes from our emotions. Our emotions drive the engine. Yes, mental toughness is vital and our thinking guides our emotions, but ultimately, it is our emotions that control performance. If we are nervous, sad, or listless, our performance will typically suffer. On the other hand, when we are energized, calm, and joyful, our performances soar. When we exhibit effective emotions, the chance of success increases greatly.

This principle, however, is not a new belief. The ancient Greeks used the term *sophrosyne* to describe the ability to value fortune and disaster in the same light. They believed qualities such as self-mastery and self-control would transcend time as essentials for a prosperous life. Today, we know that success lies not so much in ability but in emotional intelligence. Individuals who have mastered their emotions have a decided advantage over the competition.

Flying Lessons teaches parents the emotional strength and fitness program. Emotions must be continually developed as well as maintained for a successful life. The emotional strength and fitness program is composed of six key emotional strengths:

1. Emotional awareness: We must be aware of which emotions make us perform our best as well as our worst. We also need to know our strengths in order to develop our vision.

2. Emotional preparedness: Confidence comes from our preparedness. When we are emotionally prepared, we are ready for all situations. To be successful, we need to plan for the best but prepare for the worst.

3. Emotional connectedness: We should be fully engaged in the process as well as the moment. Once we are fully engaged, life gets that much sweeter.

4. Emotional bravado: We need to overcome our fears of rejection as well as our fear of looking foolish. Success stems from facing our fears head on and allowing them to catapult us to the next level.

5. Emotional drive: Success takes action and action takes boundless energy. We must power on to achieve our excellence.

6. Emotional balance: The swaying of emotions can put us out of sync with ourselves as well as the environment. Having balance gives us comfort and peace of mind.

These six emotional strengths create the structure for this book. While these strengths are interdependent, the reader does not have to follow any specific order of the strengths. (Emotional awareness is a good starting point, however). Parents can turn to a section that they believe would most benefit their son or daughter.

Sections include a series of short but entertaining chapters. An ancient proverb states, "Tell me a fact and I'll learn. Tell me a truth and I'll believe. But tell me a story and it will live in my heart forever." Every chapter contains many stories of successful people: Allow these stories to live in the hearts of your children. Not only read the chapters, but share these stories with your children at every opportunity.

The chapters are more than just entertaining stories. Each chapter concludes with hands-on activities that apply the chapter concepts to a variety of settings. Children will learn more effectively within an interactive framework, so many of the activities involve both the parent and the child. Most drills are effective for any age group. However, some drills work best for younger children, while other drills are more suited for teens. Parents can readily decide which drills fit the needs of their child. More importantly, parents should not have to force these exercises upon their children. These activities should engage your children simply because they are fun.

Like all the best experiences, *Flying Lessons* does more than just teach emotional toughness and how to be successful—it fosters character development. This book helps to instill values such as sportsmanship, integrity, and other important ethics. The hope of the author is that children will act like champions in all settings.

PART 1

EMOTIONAL AWARENESS: KNOW THYSELF

First and foremost, champions know who they are. They know what emotions drive their engine. Champions also know what makes them choke as well as what makes them play their best. Individuals like Muhammad Ali have learned to harness their intensity into a winning form. He knew how to get pumped up when he entered the ring, an essential skill for a boxer.

Emotional awareness can help people develop a roadmap that guides their life journey. Winners know who they are, where they want to go, and what it will take to get there. Christopher Reeve was one such individual who developed a vision based upon his talents and needs. Reeve's vision was to find a cure for spinal cord injuries, and this guided his every action.

Is your child aware of his strengths and true talents? Does he know how to use them? Does he know what makes him perform at his best? What causes him to perform at his worst? Has your child chosen his path?

The following section shows children how to find a vision based upon the principle of self-awareness. Once your child has a plan based on his true self, the steps of the journey are easy.

Discover Your Vision

Driving to spring training from New York, the famous baseball player and manager Yogi Berra and his wife were terribly late. They were driving all night and Yogi's wife fell fast asleep. To make up for lost time, Yogi took a shortcut that eventually turned into a dirt road, with more dirt than road. His wife suddenly awoke, very startled, and said to Yogi, "Honey, I think we are lost." Yogi, always equipped with pearls of wisdom, returned, "Yeah, but we are making great time."

Without vision, you may get somewhere, but most likely it will be a "somewhere" you don't want. However, once you discover your vision, it becomes the neon sign for guiding you to the correct path.

Vision is what drove Christopher Reeve to success as well as inspired him through his tragedies. Starting as a trained theatrical actor, he captured one of the most coveted roles in the 1970s—Superman. His rise to fame was fierce and he played many other roles that propelled him to the top of the Hollywood game.

Then tragedy occurred. During an equestrian competition, his horse stopped at a jump and Reeve fell off. He landed wrong and cracked his vertebrae at the top of his neck. His injury was so severe that he became paralyzed from the neck down. He could not even breathe without a ventilator.

But Christopher Reeve did not give up. Recalling the great visionaries he admired (including President Franklin D. Roosevelt, who challenged his scientific community to find a vaccination for polio during his presidency),

Reeve decided to make his own visionary statement. At age forty-three, Reeve said he would stand up and make a cheer at his fiftieth birthday party.

This vision guided his every move. Tirelessly, he made speeches around the globe encouraging people to give money for spinal cord research. He was a man dedicated to help find a cure.

Unfortunately, by his fiftieth birthday, the research had not progressed enough for him to stand and toast his friends and family. Even sadder was his death at age fifty-two of a heart attack. But his memory is the inspiration that drives many to continue his vision.

Wouldn't it be wonderful if your children could have a vision as powerful as Christopher Reeve's that guides their everyday actions? Wouldn't it be great if your children could have a life dream that gives them direction? What if your child could have a purpose that creates boundless energy?

Most parents want their children to have a powerful vision for their life rather than float aimlessly throughout their years. This type of guidance, however, is one of the most difficult parental tasks. The following activities can help your child to develop a vision as well as find a life path.

⇨ Develop a Purpose Statement

Almost four hundred years ago, John Donne wrote, "Any man's death diminishes me, because I am involved in mankind; and therefore never send to know for whom the bell tolls; it tolls for thee."

Today, many people are concerned with giving back to society. One of those is Coach Joe Paterno of Penn State. He is one of the most successful college football coaches of all time. Coach Paterno usually had a winning season, and so had many temptations and many offers to leave for more money.

In 1972, Paterno was content at Penn State, but making only $35,000. Then the phone call came. Bill Sullivan, the president and principal owner of the New England Patriots, offered Paterno more than $1 million if he would coach his team. He would also get part ownership and $100,000 as a signing bonus. Even by today's standards, that is a lot of money and a great contract.

Coach Paterno turned down that golden contract, however. He realized that money was not what drove him. He loves to win, but he believes in something greater than victories on the gridiron. His purpose in life is to help young adults grow in both their personal discipline as well as their educational development. This purpose statement has been his beacon for more than forty years.

To help your child discover her path, ask her to write her own purpose statement. A purpose statement is a statement about what she believes would give meaning to her life. Here are a few questions to guide your child:

- Who do you admire and why?
- What have been some great contributions to our world?
- What do you see as meaningful?
- Where do you see yourself in five years? Ten years? Twenty years?
- What contributions would you like to make to the world?

✦ Find Your Values

"I do not want to have the finer things in life," wrote Martin Luther King Jr. "All I want is to leave behind a committed life." Martin Luther King Jr. valued a committed life, a life dedicated to helping others gain their civil rights.

What does your child value?

Have him make a list of his values. These may include sports, civil rights, writing and speaking well, money. Do not judge what he writes, but let him construct his own list.

✦ Discover a Career Direction

Now that your child has accomplished two essential tasks (writing a purpose statement and writing a list of his values), the steps to discovering his path will become apparent. More importantly, these two items can help your child choose the right college major and pick a meaningful career. (While this activity can be used at any age, it may be more appropriate for teens.)

First, have your son write down five college majors or training programs that he believes he may pursue, such as psychology, business, or art. Then have him list five possible career choices that he finds attractive, such as counseling, sales, or interior design.

Next, discuss together how his choices (for a field of study as well as a career) line up with his purpose and values. The majors and careers that match up easily are the most appropriate choices. If one leads to another, without any difficulty, then these are great choices. For instance, if your son values compassion, then being a counselor would line up easily. Or if your daughter values creativity, then being an artist or interior designer is a good fit.

Conversely, those choices that have to be bent and pushed to fit with your child's purpose and values should be abandoned, because they will not work in the long term. For example, if your son values material wealth, being a teacher may not work. As a rule, teachers are not highly paid compared to other professions. While teaching is a noble profession, it may be difficult in the long term for someone who wants to make a lot of money.

Once your child has identified what is essential to him, his path will become apparent.

FIND YOUR ZONE

Sally was nervous but well prepared for the "young investigator" contest at her school. Winning this contest would mean $500 toward a college scholarship.

Sally had researched her new idea all summer long. Sally was fascinated with the fear of the number thirteen that plagues many people in our society. She had read in a book that this fear, triskaidekaphobia, stems from the Last Supper. There were twelve apostles at the Last Supper: Jesus was the thirteenth person at the table. Henceforth, people believe that bad tidings are often associated with that particular number.

As she started her presentation, her nervousness subsided. Although she was presenting to her fellow students and many of her teachers, she felt a sense of calmness. As she spoke, every word came out crisply. The sentences seemed to roll off her tongue with ease. While the talk felt like it lasted a minute, she actually spoke for twelve. She greatly enjoyed the experience and did not want her talk to end.

Sally was experiencing "the zone." Some people call it a peak experience while others call it flow. Nevertheless, this zone is the magical place where everything seems to go just right—a place we long to be but rarely reach. Every athlete, student, musician, and businessperson longs to perform in the zone state.

Athletes describe the zone with mystical tones. Lance Armstrong, the famed cyclist, said that when he finds the zone, the bike is an extension of his body. Magic Johnson, the all-star Laker, said that when he found the zone, everyone on the court was in slow motion except for him. Barry Bonds, the home-run king, proclaims that the baseball looks bigger and the seams on the baseball are clearer when he enters the zone state.

The zone happens in all settings. Real estate mogul Donald Trump says that when things go well in a business negotiation, he gets into the zone. Writers can get into the zone as well. When this occurs, the stories seem to write themselves with little effort. Teachers report that they are in the zone when their students are listening intently to every word.

Of course, parents would like to help their children find this state as often as possible. While there is no one secret to finding the zone, a major key is self-awareness. Children need to be aware of what factors contributed to getting them into the zone. Once discovered, they need to replicate those behaviors and thoughts. Then their chances increase of finding the zone again. The following drills show parents how to get their children into this elusive state as often as possible.

⇨ Know Thyself

As Shakespeare wrote, "Know thyself." Our children need to know what factors led to a previous zone state.

To help your daughter develop a greater sense of awareness, ask her to describe a peak performance (zone) experience that she has had in the past. If she never had a peak experience, ask her to describe a time in which she performed well. This experience could be in music, sports, or at school. Ask her first to write down the day and place of the event. Then ask these guiding questions:

- Did you do anything special before this event? (Did you have a big breakfast? Did you prepare a lot before the event? Was the event really important?)
- What were your feelings during the event? (Were you excited? Nervous? Energized?)
- What were you thinking during the event? (Were you confident? Were you unsure of yourself?)

- Were there any special circumstances during the event? (Were you alone? Was there an audience? Was the coach yelling at you?)

These questions act as a roadmap for your daughter to find her zone experiences again. For instance, from this exercise, your daughter may have discovered that she gets into the zone when confidence is high, and she is calm yet energized. These factors, then, should be replicated when your daughter wants to find the zone.

✪ Know Why You Choke

Not only do we need to find out what makes us perform at our best, but we also need to discover what contributes to our worst experiences. Some people call this a choking experience.

To help your daughter avoid the choke as often as possible, ask her to recall a time she performed her worst. Ask her to describe that event to you. Next, ask her very similar questions to those about the zone experience, but relate them to a choking experience.

- Did you do anything special before this event? (Did you have a big breakfast? Did you prepare a lot before the event? Was the event really important?)
- What were your feelings during the event? (Were you excited? Nervous? Energized?)
- What were you thinking during the event? (Were you confident? Were you unsure of yourself?)
- Were there any special circumstances during the event? (Were you alone? Was there an audience? Was the coach yelling at you?)

These questions create a roadmap for your daughter to know what thoughts and feelings to avoid. For example, she may perform her worst when she is nervous, ill prepared, and does not care about the event. These factors, then, should be avoided and these emotions replaced with more positive ones.

➪ Develop a Zone Log

The zone experience is unique for everyone: Your son may need to be pumped up while your daughter needs to remain calm. Everyone needs to create their own personal roadmap to the zone.

The Know Thyself drill on page 8 focuses awareness of the zone experience on only one event. While that is vital, you also should ask your child to begin a zone log. This log focuses on numerous peak performance experiences.

Buy a small notebook, about two inches by four inches, and have your daughter write down every zone experience she has, all year. Each time she is in the zone, she should record the time and place of the event. Also, have her record the thoughts and feelings that were associated with each zone event.

This zone log has many benefits. First, it helps reveal any patterns in your daughter's zone experiences. Second, when your daughter is not playing well or just not feeling great about her game or skill, she can look at this zone log for a quick mental lift. While this book will only cost pennies, it is worth its weight in gold. (Perhaps Olympic gold some day!)

BUILD ON YOUR STRENGTHS

Frank played baseball beautifully. He played first base for his high school team and was the clean-up hitter. With aspirations of playing in the Major Leagues, Frank thought he was on his way to his dream. At the start of his junior year, Frank began to notice a change in his vision—his peripheral vision was narrowing. The bad news came when the doctor told him that he had retinitis pigmentosa and would eventually lose his sight entirely.

That day came at the end of May in his junior year. Depressed and bitter, Frank wanted to retreat from high school as well as life. He thought that without his sight that he was less of a person.

Frank's dad, however, knew better and said to his son, "Frank, when one of our strengths diminishes, our body adapts and we gain in so many other ways. You will have new strengths in other areas not known to you before." And he added, "Son, you are a great athlete, so use your abilities in a sport that does not require sight, like wrestling."

Frank listened to his dad and tried out for the wrestling team in his senior year. He found that his other senses had indeed become keener, especially his sense of touch and feel, which is essential in wrestling. With much determination and effort, Frank channeled his newfound strengths into being a formidable foe on the mat, leading his team to the city championships that same year.

The good news is that we all are unique and have unique strengths. As with Frank, we just need to be aware of our strengths and use them at the right time. Once we find our strengths and use them correctly, we gain a decided advantage over the competition.

Lance Armstrong used his aggressive style at key moments in the Tour de France, and as a result, won the premier event in the cycling world for seven straight years. Initially, his style of a "go-all-out aggressive, in-your-face" attitude only worked in his early years when he raced one- or two-day events. Lance knew that he could not use this style for the long haul of the Tour de France, but needed to emphasize his strength at the key moments in the race.

Every racer in the Tour de France is given a Tour bible, a guidebook that shows every stage of the course with profiles of the route. With this as his guide, Lance created a plan that allowed him to stay close to the leaders but also permitted him to use his explosive power when needed. He developed a plan to match his great talents, which helped him become the greatest cyclist of all time.

Sometimes our strengths reveal themselves out of our adversities. Such an event happened to one of the top producers in Hollywood. Stephen J. Cannell had a terrible time in school. He couldn't read and comprehend as well as the other kids. He would spend five hours with his mother studying for a test and still fail it. Stephen concluded he was unintelligent.

Instead of focusing on schoolwork, Stephen decided to place his energies on what he was good at, and that was football. Harnessing all his effort into football, he earned honors as a running back. From football, he learned that his strength lay in his application of effort. For Stephen to achieve excellence, he needed to focus all his energies toward excellence in that task.

Later in life, he was able to transfer this strength of applied effort into his career, which ironically turned out to be writing scripts for television. Eventually, he formed his own production studio where he created and produced hundreds of scripts for successful television shows such as *Baretta* and *The Rockford Files*.

Parents should take the lead from Frank, Lance, and Stephen: Have your children use their strengths as much as they can. Martin Seligman, one of the leading psychologists in the world, supports the notion of children using their signature strengths and says that individuals who can use their strengths will not only be more successful but also much happier. The following drills help parents teach their children how to use their signature strengths in life.

✪ Find Your Signature Strengths

First, have your child make a list of her five signature strengths. A signature strength is something we do best, and could range from writing to sports to being a great listener.

Strengths:

1. _____

2. _____

3. _____

4. _____

5. _____

✪ Use Your Signature Strengths

From the above list, have your child make a daily chart and record all the times he uses his strengths during a two-week period. It may be found that he uses some strengths more than others. In fact, he may not use a few of his strengths on a regular basis.

Look over the chart with your child, and discuss the following points:

- Do you use each of your strengths every day? Do you use each of your strengths at least three times a week?
- In what areas of school do you use your strengths more often?
- In what areas after school do you use your strengths more often?
- Would you be happier each day if you could use your strengths more often?
- Why are your strengths unique?
- Are there any majors in college or training programs well suited for your strengths? (if age appropriate)
- Are there any careers well suited for your strengths? (if age appropriate)

↻ Combine Your Signature Strengths

Are there situations where your daughter can combine her strengths? If so, it may speed up her success like it did for Roger Bannister.

Back in 1954, Roger Bannister was more than just a runner vying to break the four-minute mile: He also was an astute medical student. Combining his strengths, he conducted experiments on his own physiology to understand how he could perform at his cardiovascular peak.

Roger put himself through extensive stress testing on the treadmill, driving himself to collapse time and again. Afterward, he analyzed the exhaled gas to see what elements influenced his breathing during exertion. He discovered that his peak performance occurred when he breathed 66 percent oxygen. Roger believed this was the magic formula for breaking the impenetrable four-minute mile.

The next step was to implement his findings into his training. He discovered he could attain this oxygen level if he ran at an even pace without any unnecessary movements. To accomplish this, he kept his head poised and level, looking fifteen yards ahead on the track thus promoting proper breathing technique.

By combining his strengths—his running ability and medical mind—Roger became the first human being to break the mile barrier by three-tenths of a second.

Look at the strength list again with your daughter. Does your daughter have strengths that can be combined? For instance, let's say your daughter is a talented musician. Let's also say that your daughter has talent on the tennis court. Can she use her sense of rhythm from her music on the tennis court?

An essential component of sport is rhythm, and her talent in her music may help her serve and volley game.

Conversely, can she transfer her tennis talent to her music? Perhaps she has learned how to stay relaxed during tight points on the court. She has learned that her muscles must have a certain level of tension to play good tennis, yet at the same time, her muscles must be relaxed. This same knowledge will allow her to hold her instrument with the appropriate muscular tension. Combining strengths will help your child to excel in any situation.

4

STICK WITH THE BASICS

Tony Gwynn, considered one of the purest hitters of his generation, captured eight batting titles. His lifetime batting average of .38 is one of the highest of all time. Yet even a great hitter like Tony needed to go back to the basics when his hitting went sour.

For Tony, going back to the basics meant getting rudimentary, literally. His getting back to the basic strategies involved using a tee and a Wiffle Ball. Tony believed that the sound and the spin of the Wiffle Ball gave all the needed information to get back on track. For Tony, if he hit the Wiffle Ball correctly, there would be a whooshing sound as it flew through the air. If he hit the ball underneath, the Wiffle Ball would have excessive backspin and cause a whinier-spinning sound. Tony also knew that if his hands were too quick to the inside, the ball would have inside-out spin. If his hands were too late, the spin would be outside-to-in.

If getting back to the basics was essential for one of the greatest hitters, then such a strategy should work for your children when they are struggling. But getting back to the basics is not just for sport. Focusing on key fundamentals can help with music and art as well as school work. Unfortunately, many of us forget the importance of looking at the basics when we are slumping in our performance.

⇨ Develop a Mental Checklist of the Basics

Make a mental checklist to reinstate the basics. For instance, if your child struggles with his grades, go over some fundamentals of studying for tests. This list should include such basics as:

1. Read the chapter—do not skim.
2. Underline key points in the chapter.
3. Take notes of key points in the chapter.
4. Reread your underlines as well as your book notes.
5. Spread out your study time over a few nights before the test—do not cram.

You can also develop a list of fundamentals for taking a test. These could include:

1. Relax before the test (if you have time).
2. Always go with your first instincts when answering multiple choice questions.
3. Do not leave anything blank.
4. Check your answers.

Discuss which of the key fundamentals may be missing in your son's study and testing habits. Perhaps he started with all the basics but has neglected them as the semester progressed. Sticking with these fundamentals will make your son solid as a rock when the test arrives.

Turn Weaknesses into Advantages

Theodore Roosevelt is the only twentieth-century president whose face is carved into Mount Rushmore. Roosevelt remade America. He broke up business monopolies, signed the Pure Food and Drug Act, and enacted laws that promoted industrial safety. He also loved the environment and became the first president to champion environmental causes. When we recall images of TR, we often think of a man who fought passionately for the rights of the common person.

However, TR was not always full of strength and passion. The young Roosevelt did not strike most people as promising. As a toddler, he had asthma that overshadowed everything he did. Theodore was so delicate that his parents had him Homeschooled before there was a name for that type of educational program. When he did get a chance to go out to play, the other boys bullied him because of his diminutive size and frail body.

But Theodore's frailty as a child turned out to be the impetus for his charisma and robust life. His father loved his son, and knew the boy needed to change his physical appearance. He directed Theodore to embrace a life of vigorous exercise to remake himself into a strong and muscular person.

Young Theodore vowed to turn over a new leaf and build up his body, which he did with sports and outdoor activities. He became a fierce champion of the active life. He boxed and lifted weights, long before it was fashionable to work out and visit the gym. Roosevelt became an avid outdoorsman and frowned upon anybody who was sedentary or who did not have a zest for adventure.

He brought this new philosophy into all areas of his life. Perhaps this newfound attitude led to his famous charge up San Juan Hill with the Rough Riders, a charge that helped him reach the White House.

⇨ Play Your Cards

As with Theodore Roosevelt, weaknesses sometimes can evolve into strengths with the right guidance from parents.

First, you must acknowledge your child's weaknesses. The famous French philosopher Voltaire likened life to a game of cards: We all must accept the cards dealt to us.

What cards have been dealt to your child?

Have your child make a list of five weaknesses that are blocking his achievement.

Next, discuss how some of those weaknesses can be turned into a possible strength. Perhaps your son likes to daydream, which may hurt his schoolwork. Yet he may have strong visualization skills that can be turned into some form of art skill.

Perhaps your daughter loves to argue with you, whether she is right or wrong. She loves confrontation. While that may be a hindrance to some relationships, this argumentative attitude can be a potent weapon if she becomes a litigator. Perhaps your son has high amounts of energy. This "high energy" may cause him to excessively fidget in class, leading to reprimands from his teachers. However, all this energy can turn him into a fireball on the soccer field.

6

SET YOUR FLAME

In their mock Austrian accent, the infamous duo Hans and Franz on the television show *Saturday Night Live* would declare, "We will pump you up!" While they were speaking about your muscles, we also need to mentally pump ourselves up with intensity at key times. Many situations call for high levels of "psyching up" to be successful. One such situation is boxing, and the story of Muhammad Ali illustrates how he managed his emotions in order to perform at his best.

Long before he was heavyweight champion of the world, Muhammad Ali grew up very poor in Louisville, Kentucky. One summer in his youth, he saw a blue bike at the store. He desperately wanted this bike, but his family could not afford it. To pay for the bike, Ali got a job as a box boy at a local grocery store. He worked all summer and finally had enough money to buy that blue bike. As soon as he got his bike, he rode all around Louisville, showing off to his friends and family. The very next day, he parked his bike in front of the grocery store and went to work. When finished, he discovered that someone had stolen his bike. He looked all over town for his bike but never found it or discovered who had stolen it.

But Ali has a champion mentality and he harnessed this negative energy into a winning intensity level. Each time he entered the boxing ring, Ali pointed at his opponent and said, "You are the guy who stole my blue bike!"

Great performers know how to set their internal flame. The internal flame is also known as your intensity level and it must be set at the right level to help you perform at your best. A useful analogy is turning a flame on the stove when you are heating soup. When the flame is set too low, the soup will take a long time to warm up. If the flame is set too high, the soup will come to a boil too quickly and perhaps burn or spill over the sides. To heat the soup most effectively, you need to put the flame at the appropriate setting.

If your child starts slowly on a regular basis, his flame is set too low. Indications of being a slow starter would be playing the first couple of holes in a golf tournament very poorly, losing the first set in tennis on a consistent basis, answering the first few questions on the test incorrectly, and performing the first few notes in a recital a little flat and stiff.

On the contrary, your daughter may struggle at the end of a performance or competition. Here, her flame is set too high. Probably she feels very nervous or she is trying too hard. Examples of having the flame too high are seldom being able to close out a tennis match, striking out in the latter innings of a softball game, and hurrying the pace of the music at the end of a recital.

For your children to be successful, they need to adjust their intensity level to the best level. Sometimes they need to turn up the intensity while other times they may need to lower it and calm down. The following drills will help your children appropriately set their internal flame.

↻ Know Your Flame Setting

To find the correct intensity for your daughter to be successful, first ask her to recall a time she performed her best (this is similar to the Know Thyself drill on page 8). But in this case, have her rank her intensity level from 0 to 100, with 0 being totally flat and 100 being totally revved up. Create a scale with 10-point increments and have your daughter describe each level. For instance, 20 on this scale could be described as "not motivated at all," 50 could be "somewhat energized," and 70 could be "very motivated and pumped." Once the scale is completed, have her rate the last few times she played her best.

Next, have your daughter recall a time when she performed terribly. Have her again rate her intensity level from 0 to 100 on the same scale from above. Have her rank a few real stinkers to get a good pattern.

From this awareness experience, your child should have a better understanding as to what level of intensity she plays her best and at what level she chokes. Everyone is unique. Your daughter may play her best when her intensity level is set at 40 and her worst when her flame reaches the level of 80. On the other hand, your son may perform his best when his flame tops 75 and his worst when his flame sinks to the level of 20.

⟡ Get Cooking When the Flame Is Set Too Low

If your son starts at a snail's pace, he may need to learn how to kick-start his intensity. This can be accomplished in a number of ways. First, try a "blue bike story" like Muhammad Ali, if your son has one. If he does not have a story, are there images in his past that could get him fired up? Are there any wild animals he admires that act with great energy, such as a tiger or an antelope? If so, have him use these images before the start of a competition or performance. For instance, if he is a running back, your son could envision himself as a tiger breaking through the defense. Or if he runs track, the visualization of an antelope may help the gracefulness of his motion. Have your child test out images and see which ones work best.

A good warm-up routine can also get the juices flowing. For instance, if your son is a musician, he may need to play a variety of pieces before he walks onto the stage to perform. Or he may even want to try a few jumping jacks to get his blood flowing. Have him try a few different warm-up routines to see what gets him cooking before a competition.

⟡ Be Cautious with Anger

John McEnroe, the all-time great tennis player, would use anger as a pump-up strategy on the court. When things on the court were not going as planned, he would throw his famous fits, screaming at ball boys or his favorite target, chair umpires. While this worked for John, this unsportsmanly strategy is not recommended as a way to get psyched up before or during competition.

Phil Jackson, coach of the Chicago Bulls and Los Angeles Lakers, also cautions against anger and has indicated that anger can kill your skills. Phil has mentioned that while you need to have a warrior attitude on the court, you must not lose control and erupt. He is referring to our inability to act rationally when we get too angry. Perhaps he has seen too much violence occur among players on the basketball court for virtually no reason.

Scientists have indicated that getting angry quickly and losing our temper is based on that part of the brain that helps us to stay alive in a hostile world. This was especially true in ancient, more primitive cultures. However, showing excessive anger can make us lose our focus and our ability to remain rational in pressure situations.

If your child uses anger to get pumped up, make sure that he can harness that anger in a positive way. Anger must be controlled. Out-of-control rage will probably get the worst of anyone, young or old.

♦ "Try Easy" When Your Setting Is Too High

We have all heard the old success adage: "Just give 110 percent." However, giving all you have may actually be detrimental to performance. Trying too hard can negatively affect high achievement.

In a test with Olympic runners, in the first race, their coaches told them to run at 90 percent effort in a short sprint. In the second race, they were told to give it 100 percent effort. To their amazement, they actually ran faster in the first race when they tried to hold back.

Your daughter may be giving "110 percent" when competing: She may be trying too hard, leading to her difficulties in performing. To help your daughter perform her best, she may need to adopt a "try easy" mentality. She needs to learn how to ease off the pedal when her engine gets too revved up. That is, if she is at an 80 on her intensity scale, she may need to get to a 60 instead.

Have her adopt the strategy used by Olympic skating champion Scott Hamilton. Scott said he skated his best when he adopted a mentality he called "a refined indifference"—not forcing any movements on the ice, but just letting the movements happen as they may. To "try easy," then, is to simply not force a great performance.

EXPECT THE BEST

The author W. Somerset Maugham once wrote, "It is a funny thing about life: If you refuse to accept anything but the best, you very often get it." Your expectations can create wondrous achievements. Shooting for the stars helps you become a star. It helped Annika Sorenstam dominate the LPGA, the women's professional golf tour.

Annika learned the power of expectations at a very young age. Her coach, Pia Nilsson, promoted a "54 vision." Annika expects to birdie every hole; thus she is comfortable shooting a very low score. (A birdie on every hole, one under par, would equate to a score of 54.) Perhaps this vision allowed her to shoot 59 on the LPGA tour in 2001.

But while expectations can motivate us toward excellence, they also can create a ceiling of limitation. The miracle mile with Roger Bannister is a great example. Roger was the first person to ever break the four-minute mile. However, within the following eighteen months, forty-five other runners broke that supposedly impenetrable mark.

How did all these runners increase their speed?

Before Roger's great performance, everyone believed that breaking the four-minute mile was impossible. This belief placed a ceiling upon their running performance and prevented their bodies from breaking that elusive barrier. However, after Roger's great performance, the ceiling was broken and these runners had the "I can" belief.

Henry Ford once said, "Whether you think you can, or think you can't, you're probably right." Believing you can run as fast as Roger Bannister can make you faster.

Parents need to develop an "I can" philosophy in their children. Children should believe that everything is possible under the stars. Parents also need to be aware of their own expectations for their children. The following drills focus on having effective expectations.

○ Be Aware of the Self-fulfilling Prophecy

Our expectations will likely influence our interactions and, in turn, those interactions can become self-fulfilling. Psychologists conducted a famous experiment in the 1960s that supported this point. They randomly selected certain students from a variety of classrooms and told the teachers that these students were "intellectual bloomers." They told the teachers that these particular students should show remarkable gains in the upcoming year. In reality, there were no differences between these students and their classmates. But at the end of the year, these "intellectual bloomers" had better academic scores.

What happened?

Teachers had a more effective communication style with the intellectual bloomers. The teachers used more positive facial expressions and had a more engaging posture when working with the intellectual bloomers than when working with the other students. Thus, their expectations influenced their interactions which, in turn, caused grades for one group of students to be higher than the grades for the other group.

How does that relate to parenting?

First, parents must be aware of their expectations for their children. Children have different ability levels, whether it is in science or soccer. Parents usually see the difference. But those apparent differences should not influence their expectations for any child.

Second, parents should have high expectations for their children, regardless of ability level. This will lead to interactions between parent and child that contribute to high-level performance. However, expectations should not be set so high that parents have to push their child too hard. Set expectations that are high but realistic. In that way, children will be more likely to achieve their potential.

Third, parents should avoid negative expectations. If your son or daughter has a track record of problem behavior at school, it may be easier to expect the worst. But this could cause a downward spiral to develop. For example, the child has some initial difficulties at school. The parent expects more difficulties, leading to interactions that reinforce the problems at school. In turn, this creates more problems at school.

Remember, negative expectations can be self-fulfilling in the same way that positive expectations can.

⟳ Rise to the Expectations

In a study of golf professionals, researchers investigated the percentages of putts made by professional golfers from varying locations and whether the putt was for birdie or par. Amazingly, regardless of distance, the pros made more putts for par than they did for birdies. More specifically, a ten-foot putt was more likely to be made if it was for par than for birdie.

Of course, we can only speculate the cause for such a difference. Perhaps professionals expect to make at least par on every hole while birdies are a bonus.

This same principle happens with the B student in math. These students believe that they have only B potential: They expect to get a B, while an A is a bonus. Just like the golf pros, students with this type of belief will limit their potential as well as their GPA.

If your child falls into this category—and many children do—convince your child to see herself as an A student. Help her expect nothing less. As Somerset Maugham said, if you expect to get the best, you often achieve that result.

PART 2

EMOTIONAL PREPAREDNESS: BUILD ROCK-SOLID CONFIDENCE

Events rarely go as planned. Successful people are mentally and emotionally prepared for any difficulty that may arise, feeling confident that they can overcome any obstacles in their path.

Individuals such as Thomas Edison and Serena Williams have chosen to respond to life with an optimistic outlook, regardless of outcome. They used past experiences, both failures and successes, as bricks to build for the future.

This section teaches our children how to plan for the best but prepare for the worst.

8

FILL YOUR MIND WITH
MOMENTS OF GOLD

Dolly and her family have a ritual at every dinner. Everyone must tell about one happening in their day—good or bad. However, they also have another ritual, Dolly's favorite, in which each family member gets the opportunity to describe a "golden nugget."

A golden nugget is any great or special happening of the day. It could be when you aced a hard test, or scored a goal at soccer practice, or said the right words to a friend and made her smile. Dolly thinks that the best part of this process is when you get to write down your golden nuggets in a small notebook kept next to the kitchen table. Then, if there are no new golden nuggets on a given day, one of Dolly's parents will read out loud a golden nugget from the notebook to keep the spirits of the family high.

Football great Joe Montana used his golden nuggets to create great fortune on the gridiron. In the last two minutes of the 1988 Super Bowl, the San Francisco 49ers were five points down against the Cincinnati Bengals. They needed to march almost ninety yards to score. In the huddle, Joe told his teammates, "This is just like '81."

Those words in the huddle allowed Joe and the other 49ers to recall a golden nugget: A very similar pressure situation in which they succeeded. When they were playing the Dallas Cowboys in the 1981 NFC championship game, the 49ers needed to advance the ball down the entire field in the last minutes of play. With just a few ticks left on the clock, Joe threw the famous catch to Dwight Clark for the winning touchdown. Those winning images—that golden nugget—gave them a sudden jolt of energy and bolstered their confidence, which carried them to victory over the Bengals and to another Super Bowl title.

Recalling successful experiences is key to developing a strong mental game. Individuals who can replay key successful moments in vivid detail have an enormous advantage against those who lack this skill. Here's how you can help your child fill her bag with golden nuggets.

➡ Bag a Gold Nugget

Like Dolly's family, develop a family golden nugget book. Alternatively, have your daughter develop her own golden nugget book. Suggest that she write down any times she performed beautifully, whether it was a musical piece played on her instrument or a perfect shot in tennis. But have her do more than just record it. Recommend to your daughter that she mentally pull the golden nuggets out when needed, such as during a break in a tight tennis match.

Those nuggets are bound to turn her performances into gold.

➡ Get into Print

Most successful people have scrapbooks filled with press clippings about their exploits. If your child has never been the subject of a newspaper article, encourage him to make one up (this will help your child's writing, too!).

Make a page or form on your computer that is similar to a news clipping. Have your child describe what happened in a box on the left, in the third person, as if a newspaper reporter were writing it. Then, take an action picture of your child and place it in the box on the right. Make sure he writes a catchy caption at the bottom of the picture, just like a newspaper reporter would.

If you don't have a computer available, then do the same with paper.

Seeing an article about themselves and reading about their accomplishments as though they're famous is a great way to build children's confidence.

⇨ Make a Peace Book

Most every child has memories that can promote positive emotions in the present. Ask your child to recall a moment when she felt completely peaceful and happy. Perhaps it was standing at a beautiful waterfall, or sitting at the end of a pier watching the boats roll by, or lying on top of a mountain looking at the valley below, or watching a sunset over the water. Now, ask her to record that moment. Describe it in great detail in a "peace" book.

Next time she has an anxiety-related moment such as a math test or a speech to give, tell her to read a passage from her "peace" book. This practice should help her stay calm in times of turmoil.

9

Choose Your Attitude

The Norwegian people have it down cold. They live in a usually frigid environment, yet they are a nation of outdoor enthusiasts. They have a tendency to see only the positive of their climate and have a saying that captures their perception: "There is no such thing as bad weather, only bad clothing."

We have a choice to feel great about our day, or feel like we should still be in bed. We have a choice to remain positive about events outside our control, such as the weather, or to become gloomy with each passing rain shower.

The same principle applies to our confidence. We have a choice to believe in our exceptional skills or to believe that everyone else has more talent at our job or position.

While essential to possess in any endeavor, confidence is as fickle as an eight-year-old boy in a candy store. One moment he wants the Gummi Bears and the next he wants the sour chews. A great performance can create the sweet state of invincibility. One bad shot or one foolish mistake can sour your attitude and perception of your ability.

One of the toughest mental skills is to keep that sweet feeling of confidence even when your performance takes the train south for the day. However, no matter how poorly you are playing or performing, you can always choose to remain confident. No matter how many disappointments or mistakes you make, you can still choose to taste that sweet feeling of confidence.

Ask Willie Mays, the baseball star who always had a smile on his face. A former teammate recalled how one day at the start of a big game, Willie declared to the guys, "This is going to be a great day. I'm going 4 for 4 today. No doubt about it." After Mays struck out in his first at bat, he came back to the dugout and said, "This is a great day today. I'm going 3 for 4." When he failed to get a hit in his second at bat, he proclaimed that he was going to go 2 for 4. Then he grounded out for his third at bat and made the bold statement that he was going 1 for 4. Later in the game when he was robbed of a base hit on his last at bat, he smiled and said, "Tomorrow is going to be a great day. I'm going 4 for 4."

Centuries ago, the founder of modern philosophical thought, René Descartes, wrote that we have the capacity to think whatever we choose—and to have thoughts that are self-liberating or those that are self-defeating.

This same principle applies readily to our children. They can have self-liberating thoughts that free them from the fears of everyday life or they can choose a life full of self-doubt. A parent's goal should be to make sure their children know that they have a choice to be confident and to encourage them to make that choice often. The following drills should help your children believe that they can go "4 for 4" every day, in every way.

⟡ Have an Early Morning Happy Hour

When most of us wake up, we focus on everything that needs to get done that day. If the list is great, and the time minimal, our attitude can sour quite quickly. The same goes for children and young adults.

To help your child start the day in a good mood, try this simple exercise. When your child wakes up in the morning, have her focus on three things she is thankful for in her life. It could be her health, her friends, her pet, or her family, and so forth. She will find that when she chooses to focus on these simple thoughts, her morning will be that much brighter. It is an early morning happy hour.

Conversely, if your daughter focuses on the bad events when she wakes, she is bound to create a bad mood. To prove this point, have your daughter try this experiment for two weeks. For the first week, your daughter should write down three good things (big or small) that happened to her during each day. Also, address the question, "Why did this good thing happen?" At the end of the week, have your daughter rate how much she enjoyed that week on a scale from 1 to 100, with 100 being the best.

The next week do the opposite. Have your daughter write down three bad things that happened to her each day. Again, have her answer why these bad things happened to her. At the end of the week, let her rate how much she enjoyed the week on the same 100-point scale.

Most likely, she will find that her enjoyment for the first week will be much higher than for the second week. This simple experiment will illustrate that when she chooses to focus on the good events, she will place herself into a much better mood. Or she can emphasize all negative events in her life and feel bad. The choice is hers.

10

TALK YOURSELF INTO GREATNESS

Most champions use positive self-talk. They routinely pump themselves up with the right words: Like Serena and Venus Williams, the tennis dynamic duo. While they are best known for their single victories, these sisters also play doubles and are a formidable pair, to say the least. But this one afternoon, they were losing decisively. They needed to grind it out to win this match, but Venus was not particularly focused and looked despondent about their chances of winning.

Usually during a changeover, the sisters talked about anything from movies to shopping to boys, but during this changeover, Serena gave her older sister an earful. Serena said, "Listen, I don't care what you do on your side of the court, but I'm not going to miss on my side. We will not lose this match."

Then Serena went on to say, "Look, Venus, no matter how you feel about your game, you have to show up at the court, right? You're here to play tennis after all. But you do have a choice about whether you want to compete well or compete badly. I'm going to make the choice to compete well. Why don't you do that, too?"

Apparently Serena talks herself into winning on the court. She was also trying to get her sister to feel the same winning way.

Positive self-talk can do more than help us win, however. It can even change our brain. Our thoughts create neurological impulses which stimulate the creation of new pathways in the brain. The more we think any thought, the stronger and more available the pathway becomes. So repeated positive thoughts can super-charge our brains with positive energy and help us become champions.

Positive self-talk should start at an early age. Gary Player, one of the greatest living golfers, has used positive mental talk since he was a young lad growing up in South Africa. His teacher remembers walking by Gary's classroom and seeing Gary staring intensely into a mirror, talking to himself. He was repeating the same sentence over and over:

"You're going to be the greatest golfer of all time."

Wondering how many times he'd say it, the teacher started counting: When Gary got to his hundredth repetition, the teacher gave up watching (and decided to skip the pep talk he'd planned, as Gary was doing just fine on his own). When Gary grew up, he became an all-time great, winning all four majors in his career.

Unfortunately, many children are not like the young Gary Player. Instead of engaging in positive self-talk, many children do the opposite. Tiffany, a young actress trying to break into commercials, had that problem. She played a negative mental tape in her head. Although she had a lot of talent, she never auditioned well. Before every audition, she said things like: "I know I'm going to blow it again!" and "Don't choke this audition again."

Making these destructive self-statements helped to burn a negative mental tape in Tiffany's brain. She had become her own worst enemy. One day, after listening to Tiffany berate herself, her mother asked her this question: "Who would you like to have around during an audition—someone who always calls you names and puts you down or someone who praises you and pats you on the back?"

"Of course, the one who praises me," Tiffany said.

Then Tiffany's mom told her she was her own worst enemy. "You're the one who's self-destructing your performance—no one else." With that insight, Tiffany began to realize that she was the obstacle to her potential. She stopped using negative self-talk and self-destructive tones in her communication.

Sometimes changing a negative mental tape into a positive one can happen due to a simple insight, as in Tiffany's case. Other times, the change comes with using key mental exercises. The following are a few mental tools to help your children talk themselves into excellence.

○ Develop a Best Friend's Journal

Just like Tiffany, your daughter would like to be around someone who pats her on the back before and after a performance. Your daughter must become her own best friend if she wants to achieve excellence.

To get your child started, ask her to select a small notebook, one she likes and will feel comfortable carrying wherever she goes. Then encourage her to write one positive self-statement in it each day, like:

- I have confidence today.
- I am a great test taker.
- I am mentally tough.
- I bounce back from errors easily.
- I feel great today.
- I like myself.

Encourage your child to write one of these self-statements in the morning before school or before going to bed. After writing them, encourage your child to reread a few passages every day. Making and rereading these statements will create a positive "mental tape" in your child's brain and help her become her own best friend.

○ Snap Out of It!

Give your child a bag of colored rubber bands and ask him to choose a favorite color and place that one around his wrist. Then, tell him whenever a negative thought pops into his mind, to snap the rubber band—not so much that it hurts, but enough to get his attention.

After your child snaps the rubber band, he should replace the negative thought with a positive one.

Sit down with your child and make a list of opposite thoughts together. This will help your child get a feel for how to replace the negative with the positive.

Here are some examples:

Instead of . . .	Think
I stink at soccer.	I can do it.
I am afraid.	I am fearless.
I'm no good at math.	Mistakes are okay; I will learn from them.
I do not like the coach.	Focus on myself.
I play poorly in competition.	I'm going to do the best I can and have fun.

If your son's mental tape is negative, he'll be snapping the rubber band all day long at first. But over time, the snaps will start to diminish and so will the negative self-talk.

DIRECT YOUR OWN
MENTAL MOVIES

Keith watched in disbelief as his son Charlie missed free throw after free throw. Charlie was usually great at free throw shooting—but during the championship game, nothing went in, not one shot.

On the way home, Keith asked his son what had happened.

"I tried," Charlie said, "but I kept seeing the ball miss—and it *did* miss, every time."

Images can create our reality: A literal, physical connection exists between our thoughts and actions. If you're on the free throw line and imagine the ball missing, you feel anxious, which makes your muscles tenser and your movements stiffer. As a result, you will be more likely to miss. If you imagine yourself making the shot, you feel calm, which makes your muscles looser, your movements more fluid. As a result, you will be more likely to make the basket. Our images become self-fulfilling: Visualizing success enhances our ability to perform better under pressure and succeed.

Most successful performers say they use visualization. Actors may see themselves receiving an Academy Award before filming a movie. Artists see the painting completed, even when the canvas is blank. At the start of every practice Olympic champions picture themselves on the podium receiving a gold medal. They have all described using visualization to build a winning mind-set. No one told them to visualize; they did it intuitively.

But not all people realize the importance of visualization, especially when they are young. Many children don't know how imagery can build a winning mind-set: That is where effective parenting comes in. Tiger Woods learned imagery from his father. "Putt to the picture," his dad would say.

Whenever Tiger was struggling and needed a tune-up, he would return to those basics. Before his first Masters win, Tiger pictured the ball rolling toward the cup, the crowd roaring as it fell in, his father hugging him, and wearing the green victory jacket.

Anyone can learn how to use visualization. It is a skill that must be acquired to master the mental game. Many of the drills in this book use visualization to help build a winning mind-set. The following are tips to help your child master this essential skill.

⇨ Find a Calm Spot

Visualization works best when people are relaxed. Nolan Ryan, the Hall of Fame pitcher, followed this philosophy. The night before a game, he would lie down in a specific room, close his eyes, and try to completely relax his body before he went through his mental imagery program. Once relaxed, Nolan would imagine himself going through the entire lineup of the other team, one batter at a time. He would visualize exactly how he was going to pitch each hitter as well as how it was going to feel throwing those pitches.

Designate an imagery room in your house. Make sure your child has a comfortable place to sit or lie (a chair, a bean bag, a big pillow) and let her choose relaxing music to set the mood. As the music plays quietly, read this script aloud, paying attention to your child's reactions:

> *Focus on your breathing. Listen to it. Take nice, deep breaths—in through your nose, out through your mouth. Now relax your toes. Relax your calves. Listen to your breathing—take big, deep breaths, all the way down into your lungs, then let it out. Relax your thighs and your waist. You should be feeling very relaxed now. Relax your chest and your shoulders and your arms. Relax your hands and the tips of your fingers. Focus on your breathing. Keep focusing on your breathing. Take nice, deep breaths. You should be completely relaxed now.*

Once your child is completely relaxed, which should take about five minutes, move on to the next drill.

◇ Start Easy

Your child will learn visualization more effectively if she first uses familiar images. Here is an example of a script that can be used:

> *See yourself sitting on the couch in your living room at home. See everything through your own eyes, as if you were actually there. Look around the room, see the picture on the wall, the books on the shelves, and the pillows on the couch. Be as realistic as possible. Try to use all your senses, even visualize the smell of this room.*
>
> *Now, turn on the television. See a bright red apple on the television. See it rotate. Now see a banana. See the texture and color of the banana. Rotate the banana. Now see yourself on the television, performing your favorite skill (it could be music or a sport).*
>
> *See yourself executing this skill successfully over and over again.*

Change this script to fit your child's experiences. Start with visualizations that your child knows very well and then move to more challenging images.

◇ Visualize Your Successes

The next step in developing visualization skills is to have your child pick a skill that he does well. For example, if he is a pianist and highly proficient at a certain piece of music, then have him visualize playing that piece. Here is a quick example script:

> *See yourself sitting at the piano. You feel calm and collected. As you start playing, your fingers respond perfectly. The music sounds beautiful, singing from the piano.*

◇ Work on Your Weaknesses

Have your child use the magic of visualization to become more proficient at a difficult skill. Once he has worked on his imagery skills, this step will become much easier to accomplish.

For instance, have your daughter visualize a piece of music she is struggling with on her flute. Suggest that she visualize playing this piece as if she were a concert flutist. Have her imagine that she hits every note perfectly and the sound resonates across the stage as the composer desired.

If your son struggles with his serve in tennis, have him visualize hitting serves with perfect form, peppering all the corners.

Interestingly, researchers have found that images do enhance our skill. Imagery can enhance our muscle programming (or muscle memory, as most people know it). When we want to master a skill, imagery can advance the cause.

Help your child master the skill of imagery. Suggest that he use it as much as he can. Imagery is one main ingredient to the success mix.

PLAN FOR THE BEST,
PREPARE FOR THE WORST

The Greek philosopher Diogenes was asked why he begged for money from a statue. He replied, "I am practicing disappointment." More than two thousand years ago, the greatest minds knew that bad things happen to good people. But those individuals who mentally prepare themselves for any bad tidings should be most able to respond successfully in all endeavors.

The political arena demands a prepared mind. John F. Kennedy was the first president to have a press conference routinely televised. With all the hot issues of the day like the Cuban missile crisis, the cold war with Russia, and other foreign difficulties, the press had a great opportunity to catch the president off guard. To eliminate this possibility, Kennedy sat down with a half dozen of his trusted staff and went over every possible question that he might encounter. He wanted to nullify any surprise attack from the news staff.

Being mentally prepared for negative happenings also can come in the form of visualizations. Al Oerter, one of the greatest shot-putters of all time, used visualization to win the gold medal in four consecutive Olympics, from 1956 to 1968.

Al knew that champions had to overcome continual adversity. Therefore, he visually prepared himself to perform under adverse conditions. He imagined the day of the Olympic finals, in the pouring rain. He imagined the throwing area in atrociously slippery conditions, yet he still threw with great technique. Or sometimes Al pictured having just one more throw attempt in the Olympic finals, with the Russians trailing just behind him. He had just performed poorly in his previous throws, but he envisioned responding to that adversity with a new world record on his last attempt.

Syrus, the fabled philosopher, said that anyone could hold the helm when the sea is calm. The challenge is to steer straight and clear under choppy waters. The following drills can help children navigate through the rough waters of life.

◇ Create an Adversity Plan

To prepare your child for bad events that can occur, create an adversity plan. Have your child write down a few negative things that may happen during a competition, recital, test, etc. Then, create a corresponding list of positive responses to the adversity. The following is an example of an adversity plan for a musical competition.

Adversity	Response
He is late to the recital.	He acts unhurried as he enters the stage.
He realizes one of his strings is broken.	He calmly gets another instrument from his teacher.
He makes a mistake during his piece.	He continues to play, with no visible reaction to the mistake.
The audience is making noise.	He blocks out all distractions.
His accompanist makes an error.	He calmly continues to play.

◇ Implement the Worst Ball Drill

Creating an adversity plan is only the first step. Implementing the plan is next.

Implementation can occur with visualization like Al Oerter used. Your daughter can go through the list of bad events and then visualize her positive responses to those events. If the adversity plan pertains to a music recital (as above), the young musician should visualize the list a few times each day for a few weeks before the event.

Even better is to implement adversity in real life, if possible. Payne Stewart, the Hall of Fame golfer, knew the importance of practicing for adversity. In many of his practice sessions, Payne used a drill in which he would hit two golf balls, but instead of playing the best ball, he played the ball from the worst location. Payne was preparing for how he would play his best from poor conditions. Given that the U.S. Open is full of adverse situations, perhaps this drill is one reason he ended up winning two U.S. Opens.

To be a winner like John F. Kennedy, Al Oerter, and Payne Stewart, teach your children to plan for the best but to prepare for the worst.

13

ACT LIKE A STAR

The Spelling Bee in Tallahassee plays out for ten hours. Children from all over the county enter this big event, and the winner gets a trophy and $200 certificate at the local computer store.

While it can be a lot of fun for most kids, the Tallahassee Spelling Bee can turn into a long and grueling tournament. During the final hour of last year's event, every child remaining in the contest looked tired except Suzy. She perked around on stage, looking as fresh as she had in the first hour of the contest. When the contest was over, another contestant asked Suzy how she still had all that energy and spark at the end.

"My dad always told me, 'Fake it until you make it,'" Suzy said. "I was tired at the end of the day, but I *pretended* to be bursting with energy. The weird thing is that when I acted that way, I started to feel that way!"

Her great energy was not enough to win the spelling bee, but Suzy had learned that day what all top performers have known: Whenever they step onto the field, stage, or classroom, they have to perform, no matter what. Winners aren't always motivated, eager, and confident. They can get tired, sick, and burned out. But they know that when the bell rings, it's time to put negative feelings on hold, and they do. They call forth whatever emotions will empower them to win.

How do champions turn fear into boldness or fatigue into energy?

They act—or in the words of Suzy's father—they fake it until they make it. Great acting is the ability to portray emotions. A skilled actor shows emotions with his face, eyes, hands, poses, movements—everything he does, even the way he walks, shows the audience how the character feels.

But a great actor doesn't just show the emotion to the audience—acting an emotion can make the actor actually feel it.

Psychologists have discovered that our emotions follow from our actions. People who always strut their stuff often feel confident no matter what the score is or how many opportunities they've just blown. People who act like winners feel like winners, think of themselves as winners, and are more likely to become winners than people who act like losers.

Chris Evert is a great example. She always acted confident and committed, even when she felt out of sync, weak, or nervous—or just didn't want to play tennis. But Chris never revealed feelings of weakness or doubt to anyone, especially an opponent. Instead, she showed a fighting spirit, a will to win. She always kept her head high and her shoulders tall. She roamed the court like a lioness looking for her prey. Her exceptional acting skills helped her achieve eighteen Grand Slam titles.

Unfortunately, when the chips are down, many young people act like whiners, not winners. Andrew, one of the best young golfers in Tennessee, could drive the ball three hundred yards. The best coaches taught him the sweetest swing. But Andrew was a bad actor. After every missed putt or shot, he slouched, pouted, and hung his head. His negative body language chased his confidence away. Andrew's lack of acting skills blocked his success and prevented him from fulfilling his considerable potential.

Your child may never take acting classes. She may never want to be on stage or in the movies. But to unleash the champion inside, she must believe she is a great actor and *become* a great actor. Whenever she steps into the classroom, on stage, or onto the court or field, she must act like a champion, radiating confidence no matter how she really feels. And she will become confident because the emotion she portrays is the emotion she will ultimately feel. The following exercises can help your child become the actor all champions need to be.

○ Wear the Red Shirt

Wearing something special can make children feel special. When Tiger Woods was very young, his mother gave him a red shirt. She told him that the color red would give him strength and courage whenever he wore it. Now, as part of his Sunday ritual, Tiger always wears a red shirt. When he puts his red shirt on, his confidence grows.

Take the lead from Tiger and his mom. Ask your child what clothes and accessories would help him feel the way he wants to feel.

Does your child want to feel calmer under pressure? Try something blue and discuss the calming effects of this color. Blue is known as the universal calming color.

Does your daughter need to feel happier on the court and have more fun? Try something yellow. Yellow is a bright, fun color.

Or if your child wants more confidence, try Tiger red.

↻ Enter through the Stage Door

Joe Paterno, the great Penn State football coach, told his players that the second they walked into the locker room, they stopped being students, boyfriends, and sons. They were football players and only football players; no other roles existed for them once they entered the locker room.

Encourage your child to find a trigger that helps him discard all his other roles and play only the role of a champion. Brainstorm possible triggers or acts that could kick-start the role of a champion. Here are a few suggestions to use as triggers:

- Lacing up your shoes the day of the competition
- Putting your backpack down in the classroom
- Opening your instrument case at the start of your recital
- Tying back your hair at the start of your test

Remember, your child is in charge of how he feels. Acting like a winner creates the most effective emotions for becoming a winner.

14

ENLIGHTEN YOUR GAME

John could not believe his luck when he was blessed with twins, a boy named John Jr. and a girl named Jessy. He thought he was even more blessed when they both fell in love with soccer, one of his passions. While they were both gifted in speed and agility, his twins differed greatly in attitude. John Jr. would try on every play regardless of the score. When his team was down, he would try even harder. He never gave up.

Jessy was the opposite. As soon as she made a few bad plays, it was all over. She would pout, put her head down, and stop competing, both physically and mentally.

John knew that Jessy's attitude would be a significant obstacle to success in her future endeavors, in life as well as in sports. While his son could bounce back from his mistakes, his daughter lacked a key ingredient to success—resiliency to failure.

The path to success follows many twists and turns. Individuals who ride through those pitfalls with resolve and resiliency typically will achieve success.

One of the greatest examples of resiliency is the story of Thomas Edison. His road to success was racked with a multitude of failures. Many times in his young life, he faced excessive debt incurred from acquiring new equipment and continually building a better laboratory. Also, he failed many times to sell and promote many of his important inventions. In addition, other inventors stole his designs and infringed upon his numerous patents. And the most famous Edison failure story, retold many times, is the amazing number of mistakes he made before discovering the effective light bulb.

However, Edison's resiliency to failure was built on his effervescent optimism. He did not view these failures concerning his light bulb invention as a permanent happening or as an insurmountable obstacle, but rather as pathways he no longer needed to take. He simply saw every failure as a temporary roadblock to his future success.

Jim Abbott is another optimist with great resiliency. Jim was born with only one usable hand, which can be a major problem for someone whose dream is to be a Major League pitcher. However, Jim did not give up, but developed a strategy that fit his strengths. After pitching the ball, he would quickly switch his glove to his usable hand so that he could field any possible hit. Jim honed his skills so well that he not only became a Major Leaguer but an all-star pitcher for the California Angels.

Both Thomas Edison and Jim Abbott allowed their optimism to shine on their paths to success. Most people have the belief that optimists see the glass as half full while pessimists see the glass as half empty. While this is the archetypal analogy, psychologists believe that the difference between an optimist and a pessimist is how each explains a failure event.

Optimists are resilient because they follow what is known as the TUF strategy when describing their failures. For instance, when failure comes to an optimist, they see it as "Temporary." If an optimistic student fails a math test, she believes that she was not "with it" on that test and that tomorrow will be a better day. Optimists also see failure as "Unique." Optimistic students who fail a test believe they were not good at that particular chapter, but the next chapter will be different. They will "get" the next chapter. Failure, to an optimist, is also "Flexible." Optimistic students believe that if they change their behavior, such as by trying a new strategy, failure will be less likely to occur in the near future. If they get a tutor for this next test, success is around the corner.

In direct contrast, pessimists do the opposite when evaluating failure and mistakes. First, pessimists believe failure will not change in the near future. They believe they will continue to make mistakes and fail. Second, pessimists believe that failure will happen for every situation. Pessimistic students who are not good at a particular chapter in the geometry book believe they will not understand any chapter in the book. Third, pessimists believe they have limited control over their failures: They think that nothing they can do will change failure. Pessimistic students believe that getting a tutor or studying more will not help them get better grades. For them, once failure occurs, the situation becomes hopeless.

Besides using their children's belief system as an indicator, parents also can tell whether their children are optimists or pessimists from the language they use when it comes to achievement. The optimistic child will make self-affirming statements. They make bold comments like "I can do it," "There's always a way," "I know I can beat this," and "I will get it eventually." In contrast, a pessimistic child will make self-defeating statements such as "It's not fair," "This is impossible," "I never get the breaks," "No matter what I do, nothing helps," and "This is stupid."

There is bad news as well as good news for parents when it comes to this optimism/pessimism principle. Here is the bad news. A pessimistic child has a distinct disadvantage in a wide array of areas from performance to health. For instance, pessimistic athletes perform worse after adversity as compared to their optimistic counterparts. Pessimistic students do less well in school compared to optimistic students. Pessimistic students are more likely to be depressed and get sick more often than optimistic students. In a nutshell, a pessimistic attitude is a serious roadblock to achieving high levels of excellence as well as good health.

The good news, however, is that a pessimistic child can become more optimistic. Martin Seligman, author of *Learned Optimism* and the foremost psychologist in this area, says that an optimistic attitude can be acquired with the appropriate thinking patterns. According to Seligman, anyone can relearn and change thought patterns to become more optimistic.

Even more important, researchers have found that parents have a significant influence on enhancing an optimistic attitude in their children. To create a more optimistic child, parents should emphasize the TUF points. You can do this by providing feedback after an achievement event as well as by asking specific questions that get the child to address key points. The following are strategies to help children develop the TUF mentality.

➭ Tune Up the "T"

To enhance the temporary dimension of failure, parents should emphasize the fleetingness of mistakes. When your child fails a test or does poorly in a competition, discuss that life is a series of peaks and valleys. Sometimes we find what works, lose it, and then find it again. Discuss how a bad performance is part of a downward cycle in the scheme of life. Some days are just going to be worse than others. Some days we have it and some days we just do not. Also, ask your child some probing questions about the failure experience. Here are some examples of questions that illustrate the temporariness of failure:

- Were you at 100 percent today? (Perhaps tomorrow or the next time you take the test, you will be at 100 percent.)
- What might change in the near future?
- Will you have a different teacher next term?
- Will you be studying different chapters for the next test?

➭ Urge on the "U"

To enhance the unique dimension of failure, parents should emphasize how the event was special. In sports, discuss how this team or player may not have fit your child's game. For instance, in tennis, perhaps the player rushed the net and that did not match your child's game. If the failure relates to testing, discuss how this chapter did not match up well with your child's thinking style, but the next chapter will. Perhaps the Pythagorean theorem does not click with her, but she understands pi.

Ask the following questions:

- What was it about this specific player (test) that you did not like?
- Are there any strengths that you have that will help you succeed in the future?
- How do your skills match up differently with the upcoming tests (opponents)?

↻ Foster the "F"

To enhance the flexibility dimension of failure, illustrate how failure can change by altering some behavior. For instance, if your child blew a musical recital, focus upon changing a strategy for the upcoming contest. Perhaps a change in preparation is needed. Or the child may need to practice her breathing techniques before the recital. If your child shot free throws very poorly at the last game, try implementing a pre-shot routine—a series of behaviors that a player conducts before the shot that can lead to better performance.

Also ask the following questions:

- What can we change for the upcoming contest for you to be successful?
- Is there another strategy you can implement to be more successful?
- Will a tutor help you succeed? Do you need a different coach?
- On a scale from 1 to 100, how much effort did you give? Can you give any more effort? How can you go about doing that?

When your child develops the TUF mentality, failures should begin to soften and the road to resiliency should be much easier to find.

15

IMITATE GREATNESS

Matt was frustrated. His son, Kip, towered over everyone in his basketball league, but he was timid at the hoop. Like many fathers, Matt coached his son, and like many fathers, he was hard on him. He tried yelling, he tried coaxing—but no matter what Matt did, Kip did not get aggressive on the court.

Then the two of them watched the Miami Heat play on television. Kip told his father that he admired Shaquille O'Neal. Kip admired the way Shaq dominated his opponents as he pressed toward the hoop. That gave Matt an idea: He would encourage his son to act as if he were the Shaq of his league.

Matt told his son, "Whenever you have the ball, copy Shaq. Imagine what he would do and do it." With those words and insight, Kip's behavior dramatically changed. He grew aggressive on the court as well as around the hoop and began to live up to his incredible physical gifts.

Teachers use this technique (modeling) to help their students learn a new skill or get better at an already acquired skill. It's easier for most people to imitate something they've seen than something they've read about or heard described. Seeing someone else do something can give people a visual understanding of the action. They see how all the pieces fit together, which may make it easier for them to copy the action. Modeling provides essential information—such as rhythm and timing—that is difficult to convey with words. For all these reasons, modeling makes learning easier and teaching more effective.

Studies show that imitating a role model also gives children psychological benefits. Observing someone else perform a risky move can help reduce a child's anxiety about performing the move himself. Seeing people they admire doing something can also make children want to do it themselves. The right role models increase a child's motivation.

But perhaps modeling's greatest benefit is the way it can boost confidence. It definitely helped Mike. The class assignment was to speak in front of the class about future goals. Mike, however, was petrified to speak in front of his class. In the past, he had broken out in a cold sweat and at times frozen up and forgotten what he had practiced. Before he was scheduled to give his speech to the class, his buddy Ryan got up in front of the class and spoke. Ryan was cool and calm and spoke with great passion about his future interests. Mike gained solace in how well Ryan did, and when his turn arrived, he pictured Ryan and how the class responded. Mike could not believe how well copying another person enhanced his own talents.

Here are a few methods to help your child imitate greatness.

✪ Develop a Montage of Greatness

Give your child inspiring images by making a collage together. For this activity you'll need poster board, scissors, glue or rubber cement, and magazines with pictures.

Tell your child to cut out all the people she admires. Let her choose the pictures, but as she's cutting them out, talk to her about why she admires them. You can ask questions about how this person achieved greatness.

Once she has enough pictures to cover a poster board, have her arrange and paste them on the board to create a collage of greatness. Hang this someplace where it will spark visions of greatness in her, such as over her bed or on her bedroom door.

✪ Make Yourself a Star

Sometimes the best model to emulate is you. This worked for Gabriela Sabatini. In the 1980s, Gabby was one of the best women tennis players, but by the end of the decade, she hadn't had a big win in years and was losing her enjoyment of competitive tennis.

Gabby was on the verge of burnout when her sport psychologist made a video of highlights from some of her best matches and set them to Gabby's favorite music. It looked like a music video starring Gabriela Sabatini, and it revitalized her. After watching it over and over, she went on to beat Steffi Graf in the 1990 U.S. Open.

If you have the video equipment, do the same for your child. Videotape some practice sessions or competitive situations and then edit them into a show. Pick some of the best moments and make a highlights DVD. Then encourage your child to watch the DVD before going out to practice or on stage or wherever she competes. If you don't have access to video equipment or a digital camera that records videos, then do a "success scrapbook" of photos and show it to your child. This mental strategy can promote excellence by placing the child in a confident mental state before entering competition.

⟳ Discuss Greatness

Talk to your child about what contributes to greatness. Encourage your child to pick out and describe people he thinks have achieved greatness: Artists, musicians, actors, or anyone who meets his criteria. Then ask him to find out what helped these people achieve their greatness.

- Was it great skill?
- Was it the mental game?
- Was it the ability to control emotions under pressure?
- Was it practicing hard and giving the best effort?
- Was it luck?

Once greatness is found and the path discovered, it is much easier to emulate.

16

ANTICIPATE YOUR EXCELLENCE

Jessica does not have a great memory, but she is a great test taker. She has an uncanny ability to know what will be on the test. Jessica anticipates what the teacher will ask on the test from a variety of important sources. She records what questions were asked on previous tests. Jessica pays attention to what the teacher emphasizes in lectures and notes any crossover with the content in the book. She is aware of any intonation in her teacher's voice when she gives a lecture, believing that to be a clue. She combines all this information and formulates predictions about questions on the upcoming test. These predictions guide what she emphasizes in her test preparation.

Not only does anticipation help with test taking, but it can also play a vital part in mastering any fast-paced sports. Basketball, one of the fastest-paced sports, demands the ability to anticipate, particularly when rebounding.

Whether you admired his flare or disliked his irreverent behavior, Dennis Rodman is considered one of the best rebounders in the history of basketball. While rebounding takes great agility, quickness, and fast reflexes, Dennis relied on much more than his physical abilities to dominate his competition. What set Dennis apart from his contemporaries was his anticipatory capabilities.

Dennis had a great vertical jump, but he became a great rebounder because of his ability to position himself in the right location following a shot. Dennis analyzed an opponent's shot tendency and then implemented this into a strategy for determining where and how the shot would come off the rim. For instance, when Dennis played for the Detroit Pistons in the 1980s, he had specific rebounding strategies against two of his greatest opponents, Michael Jordan and Scottie Pippen of the Chicago Bulls. Dennis knew Michael had a soft touch and the ball would come off the rim quietly, so when Michael shot, Dennis would position himself closer to the basket. In contrast, Scottie Pippen had a more forceful shot: If he missed, the ball would come off the rim quicker and harder. When Scottie shot, Dennis would position himself farther away from the basket to grab the rebound.

Quickness is also a factor of anticipation. The better anticipator you can become, the faster you will be. The good news is that quickness can be trained.

Ask Wayne Gretzky. Wayne is known as one of the greatest anticipators that hockey has ever known. He always seemed to be at the right place at the right time. It started with his dad. When Wayne was young, his father created drills on the ice for him in which he had to anticipate where his opponents would be. His dad helped him develop an "ice sense."

A few years ago, Wayne was asked what separates him from the rest of the players. He responded, "Most players skate to where the puck is, I skate to where the puck will be."

As a parent, you want your children to be great anticipators. To help them make better predictions in sports as well as in the classroom, they need to incorporate two main sources: Cues in the environment and the tendencies of an opponent (or teacher). The following drills illustrate how a parent can emphasize these two sources.

⌀ Discover Cues in the Environment

Discuss with your child certain clues that the teacher gives in regards to what may be on the upcoming test.

- Does the teacher write key words on the blackboard?
- Does the teacher say, "This is important"?
- Does the teacher clear her throat before giving vital information?

Make sure your child is aware of what cues, or in this case, clues, she can use to help predict test content, as Jessica did.

In terms of sports, discuss what anticipatory cues your child can use to help her become faster on the court or field. For instance, in tennis, the service toss gives vital predictive information. If the toss is over the right shoulder (for right handers), there is a high probability that the serve will be flat, with little spin. If the toss is above the head, then the serve should have more spin.

Discuss a variety of different situations that occur in your child's sport in which he can glean vital predictive information.

⟳ Develop an Opponent Log

Bob Feller, the Hall of Fame pitcher for the Cleveland Indians, kept a log of opposing batters. After each game, he would chart the likes and dislikes of the batters. He would log what pitches they liked to hit and which ones they avoided. To get more precise with his player log, Bob even watched the opposing team's batting practice for tips and hints.

Like Bob, encourage your child to keep a log of opponents. After each game, have your child record the subtle nuances of an opponent. For instance, in tennis your child should record whether an opponent likes to hit forehands down the line more than crosscourt. Record whether an opponent likes to serve out wide on big points or down the middle. More importantly, have your child view this log before the game to create a quicker mind on the court.

For a quicker and more effective mind in the classroom, have your child be like Jessica. Encourage your child to keep a log of what kinds of questions the teacher asks on previous tests. To help your child with the log, ask questions such as:

- Did a majority of questions concern basic knowledge or applied knowledge?
- Were the questions about names and places or more general?
- Does your teacher like to ask more questions related to her lectures or the book?

A teacher's preference for certain types of questions will tend to remain constant on future tests, and knowing these preferences can give your child a winning advantage.

PART 3

EMOTIONAL ENGAGEMENT: MIND YOUR FOCUS

Successful individuals focus their energies in the here and now. They typically do not worry about failure because that exists in the future. They do not worry about what happened in the past—that is old news.

People like Maria Sharapova, Jack Nicklaus, and Conan O'Brien have mastered the emotional strength of being connected to the present moment. They have learned to live fully in the present and focus their attention on the target, pure and simple.

Do you wonder why your child gets easily distracted at school or at the dinner table? Do you wonder why he cannot harness all his energies into one task?

This section teaches children how to live fully in each moment, and when they learn that essential skill, their moments will be much sweeter.

17

PLAY NOT TO LOSE

arents need to be careful how they communicate with their children. A true and quite humorous story serves as an example.

George Wheelwright, one of the founders of Polaroid, needed capital for his new company and asked the millionaire J. P. Morgan over for dinner at his house. J. P. had a reputation for being ornery, but he was very sensitive about his nose, which was big and red. Before the dinner, Wheelwright coached his young daughter, saying, "Don't say anything about his nose. Don't stare at his nose and please don't even mention the word *nose*." Everything went well until the very end of the dinner when Wheelwright's daughter went over to Mr. Morgan with the coffee tray and in her little voice said, "Mr. Morgan, how many lumps of sugar would you like in your nose?"

Although this story is rather old, the premise still holds true. When we focus on something we don't want, we bring attention to it. Everyone knows the classic lines about bringing attention to something we do not want:

Please don't think of a pink elephant. Think of anything else, but not a pink elephant.

What did you just think about? What else but a pink elephant? You disregard the "don't" and you think of only the pink elephant.

Psychologist Daniel Wegner calls this the ironic process theory. By telling yourself not to think about something, you can force your thoughts in the unwanted direction.

The same principle holds for playing to win versus playing not to lose.

Players who focus on playing not to lose can end up losing, which is what happened to Serena Williams at the 2004 Wimbledon championships. She was the defending champion playing a young upstart from Russia named Maria Sharapova.

Maria had a much different mentality than Serena. Maria's mentality on the court stems from her upbringing. Almost fifteen years before, her father left their homeland in Russia to take Maria to the promised land of America. Leaving the rest of the family, he came to the United States with only $700 in his pocket and very poor English skills. He risked it all so that Maria could play tennis in the hotbed of Florida talent.

Maria harnessed all that "go for broke" mentality into the final against Serena. Hitting out on every shot, she went for every line. Maria played fearlessly the entire match.

Serena, on the other hand, was playing not to lose: Serena was already a millionaire and had many championships under her belt. She had everything to lose. She played tentatively, grasping to keep her crown.

Maria, at the tender age of sixteen, played to win. The result: Game, set, match—Maria.

↻ Positive Reframing

Parents can help their children become winners by teaching them to reframe their thoughts and self-statements. Catch your children making statements that can negatively impact performance and help them replace those statements in a more effective manner. Here are a few examples:

Negative statement	Positive statement
Don't hit it into the water.	Hit it down the middle.
Don't get a C on this test again.	Just do my best.
Don't choke.	Make a smooth kick.
Don't make a mistake.	Focus on hitting all my notes.
Don't stumble in today's presentation.	Tell a great story in class.

⇨ Positive Parental Communication

Children are not the only ones who may need to reframe their communication style. As George Wheelwright found out so many years ago when J. P. Morgan came to dinner, parents need to be positive in their communication style. Simply put, keep the *don'ts* out. Speak in a style that emphasizes what you want. Here are a few examples for parents:

Negative statement	Positive statement
Don't make a mess.	Make sure your area is clean.
Don't hit your brother.	Play nice.
Don't watch television.	Go study.
Don't talk so loud.	Use your quiet voice.

When parents speak positively, they increase the chances of getting what they expect from their child.

18

BE IN THE MOMENT

"Dad, trust me, I'm trying," Max told his father after showing him his report card. "I study," Max added, "but when I take the test, my mind wanders and I lose my focus."

Max's dad replied, "The problem is your multitasking behavior. Every night in your room, you're doing so many different things at once. You're talking on the phone to your friends, playing a game on the computer, and listening to music, all at the same time."

He thought a minute and added, "Unfortunately, your concentration habits have become your enemy: This multitasking has trained your mind to become easily distracted. When you need to concentrate all your energies on the test, you can't."

Concentrating all your energies on one task is essential to performing at your highest level. Whether it is for school, sports, or music, the best performers live fully in the moment, focusing their entire energies upon one goal.

Phil Jackson, known as the Zen coach of basketball, also believes in the strength of living in the moment and teaches his players to follow suit. One of his most famous pupils, Michael Jordan, took Jackson's philosophy to heart both on and off the basketball court. Being in the here and now helped Michael stay passionate about playing hoops. He enjoyed his time on the court, inspired by new challenges and opportunities. This philosophy gave Michael the ability to feel the sweetness of the moment.

Michael has also noted that being purely wrapped up in the moment empowered him to play basketball without any self-criticism, doubt, or inhibition of any kind. When he played professional basketball, Michael did not worry about losing because failure exists in the future. His past did not exist either, allowing past disappointments to disappear. Ultimately, this approach enabled Michael to steer his emotions in the direction of excellence.

Here are a few exercises to help your children train their minds so that they can focus all their energies on the task at hand.

⇨ Breathe Well

Here is a game that not only assesses concentration but can also teach focus. First, have your son close his eyes and think only of the air going in and out of his nostrils. As soon as any thought creeps into his mind (other than the air), he has to open his eyes.

Most likely, you will find he opens his eyes within a few seconds. If so, this is a clear indication of his inability to focus.

Play the game again, but this time have him imagine white air going in his nostrils and dark air going out. Most likely, you will find that he doubles the time he can stay focused on the air.

Play the game a third time. This time have him imagine the air rolling into his nose and rolling out. (Or you can make up a few images that you think he may like.)

This game will help him build the skill of focusing on the task. More importantly, this skill will transfer to other key tasks like taking tests and listening to the teacher.

⇨ Get a Trigger

Mark Twain once wrote, "A powerful agent is the right word. Whenever we come upon one of those intensely right words, the resulting effect is physical as well as spiritual." Twain was writing about the power of words to create an effect; one powerful effect that the right words can have is improved focus.

The movie *For Love of the Game* illustrates the principle behind Mark Twain's words. In this movie, Kevin Costner plays the role of a Major League pitcher for the Detroit Tigers. Costner is older but has a unique gift: He can block out all distractions. In one scene, while he is pitching against the Yankees in New York, the fans heckle him unmercifully. However, Costner's character has learned to counteract all those distractions with a "trigger sentence." At the start of his pitching routine, he says to himself, "Clear the mechanism." As soon as he says those magical words, all the fans fall completely silent. More amazingly, all he can see is the catcher, batter, and umpire, as if they were placed within a tunnel. His trigger sentence gives him supreme focus on the task at hand.

To help your children focus more intently on the moment and be fully engaged, have them use a trigger sentence or word. An example of a trigger sentence is "Be here now," or "Focus," or they can use "Clear the mechanism," as Costner's character did. Every time they feel their mind drifting away from the moment, they should repeat this sentence. This sentence promotes the feeling of pulling all your energy back to the task at hand, whether it is a discussion at the dinner table or in the classroom or on the playing field.

The trigger can be a physical movement rather than a word. Dr. Dick Coop, a sport psychologist for many professional athletes, recommends engaging in some type of physical behavior to help a person enter into a deeper level of concentration.

Discuss with your child which physical behavior she would like to engage in to trigger a higher level of focus. Here are a few suggestions:

- Tapping the pencil on the desk three times before a test
- Bouncing the ball three times before serving in tennis
- Tapping the saxophone twice before starting to play
- Hitching your pants before hitting the golf shot

Have your child try a few. Some might work for her better than others.

↻ Savor the Flavor of Life

When we are fully engaged in the moment, the moment is that much sweeter. Being fully engaged makes our senses more sharply in tune with what we are doing.

Try this exercise with your child to prove this point. Get a Starburst candy. Any flavor will do. Have your child unwrap it and then close her eyes. Your child should then place the candy in her mouth and simply enjoy the intense flavor. Tell her to savor that intensity.

Most of the time when we eat candy, our mind focuses elsewhere and not on the flavor of the candy. But when we have our eyes closed and can completely focus on the flavor, the flavor intensifies.

Moments in time are like that as well. Each moment intensifies with flavor when we are fully engaged. Your child's life will be much sweeter when she can master this skill.

19

TRASH YOUR MISTAKES

Every time Katie made a mistake on the soccer field, she would get slower. With each error, her feet would slow down just a bit. By the end of the game she would usually be one of the slowest players out on the field.

Frustrated, Katie said to her dad, "I don't get it. I'm in great shape. So why do I feel like my feet are in molasses by the end of each game?"

Her dad answered, "It's like you're carrying a bag of bricks. With each mistake, you're adding another brick to that bag. So by the end of the game your bag weighs a ton and you can hardly move."

Katie's dad added this advice: "If you quickly let go of your errors, this bag will be as light as a feather and you will not lose any of your speed."

Jack Nicklaus, voted the greatest golfer of the last millennium by sportswriters, also understands the importance of leaving negative events in the past. He understands that past failures create negative images and those negative images hurt his future performance. One night while giving a seminar, Jack said that he never three-putted the last hole of a golf tournament. (When a golfer hits the green, he wants to one-putt or two-putt; three-putting is a bad event in the golf world.)

When an audience member mentioned that he saw Jack just last week on television three-putt the last hole of a tournament, Jack again responded that he never three-putted the last hole of a golf tournament. Whether or not he three-putted is not the point. Jack had eradicated that negative putting event from his mind. He only focused on the past in a positive light, and thus he no longer carried that negative baggage with him to the next tournament.

Unfortunately, many children are like Katie and not like Jack Nicklaus.

Instead of selective amnesia of the bad events, most children engage in rapid recall of bad events. For instance, some young musicians will not remember all the correct notes they played in practice but will recall the notes they missed. Then when they are playing the piece for an audience, they think only about how they messed up those particular notes earlier in practice. Unfortunately, recalling this negative baggage decreases their chance of playing beautifully under pressure.

Parents tell their children that forgetfulness is a bad trait. It's true that forgetting your homework or forgetting the time of your team's practice can create havoc. But sometimes forgetfulness can be a desired quality, especially when it concerns your history of errors. The following drill teaches children how to develop selective amnesia and forget bad events.

♢ Rid Your Mind of Negative Trash

Bruce Lee, the famous martial arts expert, implemented an ingenious technique for ridding himself of previous mistakes or unwanted thoughts. When a negative thought entered his mind, he wrote it on a piece of paper and wadded the paper into a tight ball. Then he threw the paper into the trash can. He would then visualize the trash can catching on fire, completely ridding his mind of the negative event.

Encourage your child to do the same thing. First, discuss with her some of the negative events in the past that should be forgotten such as:

- I messed up that easy note in orchestra class.
- I flubbed that answer on the test.
- I messed up that easy forehand winner.

Then tell your child to write down these negative thoughts she's had recently, crumple the paper up, and throw it into the trash can. Then encourage her to say, "In the trash can!" whenever that thought creeps back into her mind. Urge her to use this mental tool each time to rid herself of unwanted thoughts. Such a technique will help kick all those negative thoughts and past mistakes out of her mind.

20

QUIET THE MIND

A centipede and a worm were in a race. The centipede with all its legs could easily outwalk the wiggling worm. However, the worm was very smart and knew how to prevent the centipede from winning. At the start of the race, the worm asked the centipede how it could possibly move all those legs in perfect order, one right after the other. As soon as the centipede thought about how to walk, all its legs got tangled together. The worm then wiggled past the centipede to victory.

An action or behavior that normally is automatic can be completely disturbed when we place our attention on it. Think about this. Most of us are great typists, but we do not pay attention to where the keys are on the keyboard. We just let our fingers do the walking. But if we begin to think about where each key lies on the board, our motions become stunted and slowed.

The same principle could be applied to a pianist. After practicing a piece for hours on end, the fingers of the pianist begin to have minds of their own and move from one key to another, playing effortlessly. If you were to ask the pianist to focus on a certain key in the piece, the song would lose its rhythm and become disjointed.

A perfect example of this phenomenon ruined the career of Ralph Guldahl. Ralph was on top of the golf world in the late 1930s. He had won the 1937 and 1938 U.S. Opens and the 1939 Masters. According to Paul Runyon, one of his contemporaries, Ralph had control over the ball that was unmatched by anyone. Given his dominance, a publisher asked him to write an instructional golf book. The problem was that the golf swing came very natural to Ralph—he did not have to think too much about swinging his club. To write his book, he had to break down his swing piece by piece and analyze his every move. As a result, when the book was finished, so was his game.

What happened to Ralph Guldahl? The easy answer is that Ralph suffered from what is known as "paralysis by analysis." Sport scientists have recently discovered that when we overthink or overanalyze, we stimulate the part of the brain that can lead to choking in a performance. More specifically, when we think too much, our left brain takes over and our performance is stifled.

Branch Rickey, the former owner of the Dodgers, once said, "A full mind is an empty bat." When we fill our mind with too many thoughts, we cannot swing. To have a quiet mind yet full bat, parents need to teach their children how to suppress their analytical thoughts. The following drills help children learn this important skill.

◇ Don't Force Your Character

Conan O'Brien arrived in Los Angeles in 1985 to take a job as a comedy writer. He was also trying to get work as a performer. In one class that changed his life, he was asked to improvise a scene. However, instead of improvisation, he planned every line in his head. He wanted to show off his comic genius to the group.

Conan's instructor yelled, "Stop thinking so much." That advice left an indelible mark on his future endeavors in show business. Now, instead of mentally writing ahead to find a funny place, he quiets his mind and lets the funny moment just happen. Thinking less and reacting more has proven to be the mantra of his career.

If your son is trying his hand on the comic circuit, then he should try to implement this "Conan" principle. Instead of writing out the script and acting it on stage, he needs to get into the "just respond" mode.

But this principle is not just for acting. It applies to life. Your child should not force any conversation with another person but rather just react honestly and spontaneously to people. With this style of communication, no one will think your child is forcing his character.

⇨ Become Reactive

Jason had a beautiful three-point shot. He could make threes from any-where on the court. Interestingly, he stunk on the free throw line. At times, he would even miss the rim with his free throw.

In basketball, the free throw is quite difficult under pressure because you have so much time to think. In contrast, you react when shooting a three-point shot.

Have your son develop a routine that promotes a reactive mind. As an example on the free throw line, your son could bounce the ball once, look up at the rim, bounce the ball again, and as his eyes begin to gaze at the rim for the second time, he shoots. The sequence promotes a quiet yet re-active mind. This reactive routine helped Jason to become a "sure shot" on the free throw line.

Reactive routines can be created for any sport, from golf to baseball to tennis. When your son gets reactive, he will find his game.

⇨ Transition into a Reactive State

Carl Lewis, the famed track and field star, exemplified a transitional thought process, going from thinking to reacting. At the start of every race, Carl first focused on what he wanted to accomplish and how he wanted to run the race. Then he would clear his mind and let his body respond to the race.

Sometimes we need to think analytically at the start of our perform-ance, but then we must shut off the thinking process and just respond. Such a transitional routine could be accomplished in golf. As an example, your son takes his first practice swing, thinking about a specific swing thought. He then takes another swing visualizing the feel of his movement. In his third practice swing, he focuses solely on his target.

○ Play Red Light/Green Light

While your child should diminish his analytical thoughts, at times it will be necessary to focus on the mechanics. When your son's game takes a nose-dive, he will need to self-regulate and fix it as soon as possible.

Unfortunately, most people want to analyze what went wrong after one missed shot or play. That is far too early. Sometimes our timing is a bit off and we must continue to trust our game instead of discover its faults.

If your son has a tendency to analyze his game too quickly, try the drill called red light/green light. For instance in tennis, after one missed forehand, your son is still in the green light zone. He is not to analyze anything about his game. If he misses two easy forehands, now he is in a "yellow light" mode. He is not to analyze anything but remain cautionary about his game.

When he misses three easy forehands, he is now in the "red light" mode and he must analyze his forehand. Once he discovers the problem and subsequently fixes the issue, he must go back to his reactive state, shutting off his analytical mind once again.

21

DISCOVER YOUR CREATIVITY

Albert Einstein was one of the greatest minds the world has ever known. His contributions to science, such as his theory of relativity, changed the future of our world as well as created a new philosophy of our universe. The president of Britain's Royal Society once commented that Einstein's theory was perhaps the greatest achievement in the history of human thought.

While history is riddled with great minds who made significant contributions to science, many academics have pondered why Einstein's genius stands above all others. While Einstein could easily analyze the physics of his day, most people have emphasized that his creative genius was his greatest gift.

Einstein called his way to discoveries "combinatory play." He first had periods of creative daydreaming and then put them to work, discovering new solutions to old problems. One of these playful visions led to his realization that time and space were curved, a new revelation that changed the course of physics.

Many people can analyze situations, but very few have creative genius, and it is probably this talent that gives a person a decisive advantage. One of the most creative people who ever walked down a fairway is the Hall of Fame golfer Seve Ballesteros. Seve has one of the greatest short game minds of all time and he can create magic around the greens like no other. Seve has said that he likens his artistic powers around the green to hearing tunes being played by his clubs. He understands the notes that his clubs are playing, which allows him to compose the melody needed for each shot.

Luckily, creativity can be harnessed. Dr. Win Wenger, author of *The Einstein Factor*, said that many geniuses are normal individuals who have developed some technique that promotes a more sophisticated perception of their world. The following exercises will help your children tap into their creative flow.

⇨ Do the Twain

One of the joys of visiting Hartford, Connecticut, is touring the Mark Twain house. Built at the end of the nineteenth century, it is a majestic craftsman house, glorious for any generation. Once you enter the house, you see all the unique pieces of furniture and artwork acquired on Twain's worldwide travels.

As in most tours, each room's unique features are described. When you enter the "after dinner" parlor, the docent points to a variety of interesting objects on the mantel above the fireplace and then explains a Twain family ritual. In front of his children, Mark Twain created a new story every night using those same objects. Some nights the story dealt with dragons and princesses while other times the story focused on the mighty Mississippi. But there was always a new adventure with the same main characters.

Do the Twain family ritual. Bring out a few interesting family souvenirs, place them on the table or fireplace mantel, and ask your child to create a magical story using each piece. Use the same pieces another night, but have her create a new story. (Of course, you can try it as well.)

In weeks to come, use different objects and repeat the process. Perhaps this exercise will create another free-thinking artist.

⇨ Bowl Your Creativity

In this drill, write down a list of fifty nouns, such as *bike, car,* and *house.* Then make another list of fifty adjectives, such as *happy, sad,* and *angry.* Write the nouns on blue paper and the adjectives on green paper and then cut each word out. Place these small pieces of paper into a bowl.

Now, have your son grab three blue pieces and three green pieces of paper. Using these six, he has to make up a story with all the words. The next night, let him "bowl" his creativity again.

◇ Write on the Right Side

Find a picture that your daughter can easily draw. Make a copy of this picture. Then turn the first picture upside down and have your daughter draw this image. Tell her not to try to rotate the picture in her mind, but simply draw it as is. Then get the second picture (which is identical to the first) and have your daughter draw it right side up. Discuss the two pictures afterward. Together, you will probably find that she drew the upside down picture more artistically. When the picture is upside down, people typically are not analyzing their technique, but rather just allowing creative energy to flow freely.

◇ Make Up Dialogue

This drill can be great fun for both you and your child. Turn your television to a show that you have not seen. Pick a show that has two characters on the screen. Then turn off the sound. Next, begin to make up dialogue for the two characters. Just go with it and have fun. You will be surprised how interesting and entertaining the two of you can make a show. And this game, like the other exercises described, will play up your child's ability to create.

DIAL IN YOUR FOCUS

Will always hit well at the start of a baseball game. If you analyzed his batting average, it would be .350 for the first six innings and .100 for the last three. Will's problem was that he felt mentally drained at the end of a game, which influenced his great decline in performance. He started his games with a roar, but ended with a thud.

Will's problem stemmed from his lack of a concentration routine. He needed to develop a system that allowed him to remain fresh throughout the game. With a concentration routine, his hitting would soar at the end of the game, and so would his batting average.

Picture concentration like a reservoir of energy. If the floodgates on this reservoir are wide open, this energy will empty quickly, causing you to burn out. To conserve these mental resources and perform at your best, the floodgates should open only for a short period and then close for a reaccumulation period. Will had his concentration gates wide open for the entire nine innings. By the end of the game, he had nothing left in the reservoir.

In addition, picture concentration as waves of mental energy. Just like the waves of the ocean, your concentration will start slow, gradually build, and then crescendo. To concentrate at the highest levels, you must allow your focus to build and then peak at the right moments. If you can get your concentration to peak at the right moment, your performance also should peak.

These principles of concentration can guide parents in developing effective concentration routines for their children. The following drills incorporate these principles.

↻ Dial It In

Let's say you have a child who is a punter on his Pee Wee football team and loses focus when he is on the field. Applying the principles of concentration will help the parent develop a routine for him that increases his focus.

First, encourage your child to picture a dial on the gates of his concentration reservoir. The dial controls the amount the gates will open. When your son's team is on defense, this dial is set at 1. The gates are only slightly open. You also might encourage him to have a trigger sentence for this dial setting such as "The fun zone." He is just enjoying the game.

When your son's team gets the ball, he needs to shift his dial to 3. Here he is focusing a little more intently on the game. Your son should have a trigger sentence for this dial setting like "Time to focus."

When it is third and long, the dial should shift to 6. He needs to get ready to head onto the field in case his team does not make the first down. Your son could have a sentence here such as "Get ready."

When it becomes fourth down and a punt is called, he needs to shift his focus to 9. As he jogs onto the field, his trigger sentence could be "Time to punt."

Right before the ball is about to be snapped, his concentration should be surging. He needs to peak his focus and set the dial at 10. A trigger sentence like "Go time" would work in this instance.

After the punt, and when his team goes on defense, he should shift his focus back to 1 and enter into the fun zone again.

This routine will help your child stay fresh and peak at the right moments throughout the game. But such a routine is not just for punting. It could be used for other sports such as hitting in baseball; your child would start with low levels of concentration in the dugout and change to surging levels of concentration when entering the batter's box.

↻ Reaccumulate Your Mental Energy

Besides peaking at the right moments, we also need to have a concentration routine that helps us reaccumulate our energy. Our mind works better when we follow a certain biological rhythm. We need to have waves of high intensity work followed by a recovery time.

Suggest to your daughter that when she is working on a project that she focus, at the most, for about forty-five to fifty minutes. Then she should take a fifteen-minute break. This recovery time should consist of low-energy activities such as taking a walk, stretching, or perhaps just listening to music. These fifteen minutes are essential for your daughter to recharge her batteries and refuel her concentration reservoir so that she can keep going and be productive for the rest of the day.

23

MAKE IT ROUTINE

A scene in the movie *Shakespeare in Love* shows the young Will Shakespeare struggling to complete his play *Romeo and Juliet*. But before he starts writing, Will blows on his hands, spins around twice, grabs his chair, and sits down abruptly. Then he begins to write his famous love story.

The young William Shakespeare portrayed in this movie is engaging in a preperformance routine, a series of behaviors leading up to the performance. Unlike superstitions, which are just beliefs we carry about our world, routines prepare our mind and body for an upcoming task.

Athletes are known for their unique routines. Jimmy Connors, the all-time great tennis player, bounced the ball four times very quickly, grabbed the ball for a split second, and then bounced the ball four times again very quickly. Matt Freije, the Atlanta Hawks player who was an All-American basketball player at Vanderbilt, has a unique bouncing routine at the free throw line. Twice before he shoots, he bounces the ball so that it spins back to him. Sammy Sosa, the all-time great slugger, crosses his chest with his fingers and then looks to the sky before he enters the batter's box.

These are just a few of the examples found in sports. Turn on the television and you will see that most athletes engage in some type of preperformance routine. These routines serve a purpose. First, many of them involve a breathing response and this can promote fluidity and rhythm. Second, most routines include some type of visualization concerning the outcome of the shot, which promotes confidence. Third, routines are highly consistent. Most are conducted before the performance in a fixed amount of time. Effective routines do not vary, regardless of setting or situation. Such consistency helps bring a sense of calmness to pressure situations.

Routines help us succeed because they are disciplined patterns of thinking and acting that promote our ability to respond to an event more effectively. While routines help us deal with the pressures in sports, they also can be applied to everyday situations. The following drills illustrate how to develop productive routines in children.

♢ Create a Writing Routine

Most individuals are not like William Shakespeare. Many of us have a difficult time creating imaginative sentences and stories. To help promote this creative side of life, develop a writing routine with your child. Such a routine will put your daughter into the right frame of mind. For instance, a writing routine for her could include the following steps:

1. Exercise for about fifteen minutes (exercising helps blood flow to the brain, which can make us more creative).
2. Take three deep breaths.
3. Tap the desk three times.
4. Start writing.

Also, many writers pick a block of time to work. Their mind has been programmed to write and be creative at this time. Possibly for your daughter, a specific time after school may be a good pen time.

♢ Run with a Routine

Routines can be created to help your son become a better runner. Let's say your son is training for an upcoming fitness test at school that involves a mile run. An effective routine would be to have two easy days, then a hard running day, followed by two days off. For instance, he would run two miles on Monday and Tuesday, run four miles on Wednesday, then take two days off to rest and start the routine over again. This routine will give your son the heart of a champion.

➪ Try a Test-Taking Routine

Many great athletes have warm-up routines. Vijay Singh, winner of three majors and one of the best players on the PGA tour, has a distinct warm-up routine he uses on the range. First, he swings a heavy weighted club. Then he takes some practice swings with a towel placed under his armpits. Then he removes the towel and takes some swings with the wedges. After he feels warm, he takes swings with his nine iron and progressively moves up his clubs, finishing the progression with the driver. At the end of his session, he finishes with some easy wedges.

Follow this same philosophy to help your daughter develop a routine for the days she takes a test. This may include the following steps:

1. Read her notes before breakfast.
2. Eat one of her favorite breakfasts (a little reward on these days).
3. Reread her notes after breakfast.
4. On the way to school, listen to a "test-taking" song, a pump-up song that she listens to only on test day.
5. Ten minutes before the test, do some relaxation exercises, focusing on taking deep breaths.
6. When the teacher hands out the test, say, "It's go time."

Such a routine will place your daughter into a disciplined state of mind that helps her to conquer each test, and she will face a lot of tests throughout her school years.

➪ Develop a Post-Shot Routine

A post-shot routine is a series of thoughts and behaviors after the shot has been accomplished. This could happen in basketball, golf, tennis, or any sport where there is a slight delay before the next shot. Also, a post-shot routine is usually completed after a very poor shot, helping to clear the mind of negative images.

An effective post-shot routine has four steps. First, it encompasses an analysis of the cause for the poor shot. Second, there is a repeat of the movement (without the ball), but this time with the desired correction. Third, the player visualizes the desired shot and the routine completes with a self-statement that encourages the player to regain focus on the present. For instance, if a tennis forehand found the bottom of the net, the player first decides the cause (for instance, too much wrist). Then the player takes a shadow forehand swing with the desired stroke mechanics. The player then imagines where he originally wanted the ball to land on the court, and he finishes the routine by saying, "Next point."

A post-shot routine allows the player to leave a poor situation with a good feeling, leading to higher levels of performance.

PART 4

EMOTIONAL BRAVADO: BE FEARLESS

Most of us turn away from the possibility of failing. Or when we do have to face failing, we typically play guarded. This creates an overprotective and close-minded attitude. We cannot be our creative and innovative best when we operate out of fear.

Winners have emotional bravado. They fear not. When they do face a difficult situation, they channel that energy into a positive force. Individuals such as Mel Brooks, Bill Russell, and Jennifer Capriati engage in a fearless attack, facing their fears in order to reach the top of their game. More importantly, champions often risk failure to discover who they truly can become.

Does your child take important risks? Does he seek out challenges? Is he willing to fail and learn from those experiences? Does she know how to channel her negative energy into a positive force?

This section sheds insight on how your child can use fears and failures to propel him to the next level. You will learn how to help your child to fear less and fail forward.

24

FACE YOUR FEARS

When making the movie *Blazing Saddles*, Mel Brooks was concerned about one of his scenes. This was a comedy with cowboys doing crazy things like sitting around a campfire eating beans and passing gas. But Mel feared that having cowboys beat up an old lady would be taking his comedy just a step too far. He was considering cutting this scene out of the movie. Then one of his friends on the set told him, "Mel, if you are going to step up to the bell, ring it."

After his friend delivered that poignant message, Mel reflected upon it for a few moments, yelled for the cameras to roll, and, not surprisingly, the scene turned out to be one of the funniest in the movie.

From then on, Mel "stepped up to the bell" whenever he agonized over a decision about a scene in his movies.

Gymnast Peter Vidmar stepped up to the bell in the 1984 Olympics, although eight months before the event he was wracked with fear. It started at the World Championships in Budapest, a tune-up for the upcoming Los Angeles Olympic Games. During the World Championships, he had a lock on second place going into the finals. Peter believed that if he nailed a tricky maneuver at the start of his routine, he would be the new world high-bar champion. The move called for him to swing around the bar, let go, fly straight over the bar into a half-turn, come back down, and finally catch the bar. This feat was not easy, to say the least.

He missed the bar coming down during this move and fell flat on his face. He blew it. In his own words, he choked.

After that competition, Peter wondered if he would ever handle the pressure of the Olympics. Would he crack again? Did he have the goods?

Peter learned from that experience to meet his fears head on and never take anything for granted, especially risks on the bar. Instead of taking that move out of his routine in Los Angeles, he practiced the maneuver repeatedly for the next eight months.

When Peter overcame his fear of falling and ultimately failing, he ascended to the top of his game. He kept the move in his routine and won the silver medal in the all-around competition as well as the gold medal on the pommel horse.

Eleanor Roosevelt once said, "If you run from fear, if you deny its existence, it will chase you, track you down, and grow in size with each step." Fear follows everyone: How you react to it can help make you a champion. Parents should take the advice of Eleanor Roosevelt and help their children face their fears instead of run from them. The following drills can help your children deal with their fears.

⇨ Take One Step at a Time

Have your children picture this image: They are walking on a ten-foot-long wooden plank on the ground. Their goal is to walk across the plank without falling. The plank is just wide enough for one foot at a time to cross it. Ask them if they were nervous when they crossed the plank.

Now have them change the image. They are walking on the same plank, except it is one thousand feet in the air on a construction site. They have to walk across the plank to get from one building to the next.

Ask them how their emotions changed in regards to the walk. In most cases, they will be much more "nervous" walking on the plank that is one thousand feet in the air. Likely, their thoughts are not on crossing the plank but rather on falling.

Now, suggest they use the same image again, except their whole focus is upon one step at a time to cross the plank; that is their only thought— one step at a time.

Ask them how their emotions changed with this focus. In most cases, they will feel less nervous about crossing the plank.

Focusing on the process helps to take our thoughts away from failing, or in the previous example, falling off the plank. When we focus on taking one step at a time, we are less apprehensive about the outcome and ultimately less fearful. Engaging in the process allows us to control our emotions.

To reduce the fears in your children, suggest that they focus on the process of the journey instead of the outcome. For instance, this would include focusing on each question of the test instead of the test grade, focusing on one shot at a time on the golf course instead of the score, and focusing on giving the speech instead of how their peers will react to it. When children are engaged in the process, they have more control over their fears and nervousness.

↻ Act as If

Like Mel Brooks, most of us are continually in the throes of making important decisions. Many of us are afraid of making the wrong decision and, as a result, we never make a choice. The same can happen with your children. If they are afraid of making the wrong decision, they may procrastinate. When you spend too much time analyzing the choice, you can freeze up and never choose.

To overcome this problem, suggest that your children "act as if." Let's say the decision for your teenager revolves around choosing the right college. Suggest that your daughter visualize different colleges or training facilities she plans on attending. (Perhaps she can first take a virtual tour of the campus on the computer.) Have her visualize going to class and meeting new friends at each college. The visualization that makes her feel most comfortable is most likely the right choice.

↻ Look toward Others

According to psychology research, one of the best methods of overcoming fears is to watch someone similar engage in the act. Use this principle with your child to overcome her fears.

For instance, if your child is afraid to engage in a certain routine in her gymnastics class, see if you can have someone similar to her do the routine first—a girl of similar age, build, and stature. Or better yet, film the routine of the girl and have your daughter watch the film a few times. The same principle can be applied to music, public speaking, or a spelling bee. Observing someone similar can breed confidence in your daughter that she too can accomplish the same feat.

FAIL FORWARD

Erma Bombeck, author of humorous books such as *The Grass Is Always Greener over the Septic Tank* and *If Life Is a Bowl of Cherries, What Am I Doing in the Pits?*, was not always one of the most successful writers in America. In fact, she failed many times. While giving a speech to a group of graduating college seniors, Erma mentioned that she was not on the podium because of her successes but rather due to her failures. She told the group she had made a comedy record listened to by only a few people, made a sitcom that lasted about as long as doughnuts do at her house, and had written a Broadway play that never saw the light of Broadway.

But those failures changed her life. Erma likened failure to being a ship. While a ship is safe in port, it is not meant to be there. A ship is made to go out in rough waters. If you are not failing, you are not trying anything different. You are not challenging yourself. All her failures allowed her to find greener grass somewhere else.

Is your child afraid of failing? Are your children not extending themselves and risking disappointment? Are they playing it too safe? Are they avoiding the rough waters in life?

We fear failure because we do not like to look foolish. If we take risks, there is a greater chance of failing and looking foolish. Thus, many of us avoid challenges and important risks in our life.

Here is a simple test to evaluate the fear of failure in your children:

1. Get a tennis ball and place three trash cans at distances of two feet, eight feet, and twenty feet from a given mark.

2. Tell your children that the goal of the game is to land as many balls in the trash can as possible. (If it bounces out, it still counts.)
3. Then ask your children from which distance they would like to shoot the tennis ball.

If your child picked either two feet or twenty feet, he may have a greater tendency to fear failure. Two feet is a sure deal: Your child will not miss from this distance. Twenty feet is too hard, so there are no expectations. In both cases, your child will not look foolish and thus, his fear is reduced.

But your child may miss several shots from the distance of eight feet. Choosing this distance is not playing it safe and indicates that your child likes challenges and does not fear failure.

Being afraid to fail is a sure roadblock to your child's ability to achieve his potential. The following drills should help your son or daughter overcome the fear of failing.

⟳ Depersonalize Failure

Erma Bombeck said that one of her keys when she failed was to depersonalize it: "You are not a failure. You just failed at doing something."

The same message could be taught to your children. They are not failures, only their actions failed. Make sure they know this.

⟳ Share the Experience

Did you know that playing a musical instrument solo produces the greatest level of anxiety?

The fear of making a mistake on stage, and the belief that everyone will notice when you do, can produce a nerve-wracking experience.

Even the great cellist Yo-Yo Ma has acknowledged that he still gets nervous when playing before an audience. But Yo-Yo Ma has developed a mental strategy to quell his fears. Instead of trying to prove himself to the audience, he focuses on sharing the music with the audience. Yo-Yo believes that sharing is a much better way to communicate with his audience than proving.

Follow Yo-Yo's lead when it comes to reducing fear of failure in your child. If your child is a musician, discuss how he can share that experience with others. Explain that the music is a gift to the audience. Discuss how the music brings pleasure to the audience and puts them in a better mood. Deemphasize the need to demonstrate competence and to show off his talent.

⇨ Create a Failing Forward Journal

An ancient Buddhist proverb says, "The arrow that hits the bull's eye is the result of a hundred misses." We must embrace our mistakes as a way to progress.

Daria Hazuda, scientific director at Merck Pharmaceuticals, loves to fail. Hazuda says, "A failed experiment is actually a rich source of information." In her business, failures can be the most potent weapon to answers. Failed experiments often synthesize information into new, exciting research.

Unfortunately, most people do the opposite and avoid failure at all costs. The irony is that the more you fear failing, the more mistakes you will make. This fear causes nervousness, which in turn, can diminish performance. Thus, if you change your viewpoint of failure, mistakes should be diminished. When you view failure as a positive experience rather than a negative event, you are bound to make fewer errors.

Mahatma Gandhi was exemplary in his attitude toward seeing failures as a positive experience. Gandhi saw his life as a set of experiments, with each experience helping him find his path to self-realization. He reflected upon each failure, learned from it, shared what he learned with others, and then jumped into his next action with even more vigor.

Creating a "failing forward" journal will help your child reflect upon failure in a positive light. In this journal, have your child write down five mistakes she made at her last competition, practice, test at school, or other activity, then what she learned from each mistake. This process will help her stop dwelling on her previous mistakes and focus instead upon the knowledge she gained from the experiences. Writing what she learned in the journal is only the first step, however. To improve upon these skills, your child must use this knowledge. The legendary basketball coach John Wooden once said, "Failure is not failure unless it is failure to change."

26

Pen a Nickname

Lori had become one of the best junior tennis players in the country by the age of fourteen. She could pound her ground strokes and hit outright winners with both her backhand and her forehand. However, Lori was quite small for her age and did not like to come to the net. She believed she could easily get passed, due to her size, so she would just camp out on the baseline to win matches.

Her father knew that for Lori to get to the next level, she needed to play much more aggressively and charge the net. One weekend, while taking a break between sets and discussing strategy, Lori's father asked her if she knew what a stealth bomber was. Lori said, "Yes, it is that plane that cannot be detected by radar."

Her father said, "Okay, from now on, your nickname is Stealth—and I want you to feel like a stealth bomber whenever you drive to the net. Just remember your nickname—you'll slip in under the radar, just like a stealth bomber." Her father wanted Lori to believe that her size was an advantage at the net, not a disadvantage, and this nickname did just that.

While some nicknames are playful and funny, the right nickname can promote confidence, enhance a jovial attitude, or even change a destiny. Ask Orel Hershiser.

It was May 1984, Orel's first year in the majors. He was carrying a 2-2 record and his ERA was a terrible 6.20. After one close loss, Ron Perranoski, the pitching coach, told Orel that Tommy Lasorda, the famous L.A. Dodger head coach, wanted to see him in his office. No person had intimidated Orel like Tommy Lasorda. While he was a passionate leader, he could be brash and loud when he wanted to make a point. Verbally, Tommy took no prisoners.

At the meeting, Lasorda told Orel that he was not angry at his mechanics but with his attitude on the mound. Lasorda said that Orel looked fearful on the rubber. Lasorda began to berate his rookie, "Who do you think these guys are at the plate? Babe Ruth? The Bambino is dead!"

Then Tommy changed his tactics: He told Orel that he had the right stuff or he wouldn't have been brought to the majors. He said he believed in Orel, but that Orel needed to take charge, attack the hitters, and be a bulldog on the mound. With that insight, he shouted, "And so from now on, I am calling you Bulldog!"

As he walked to the mound at the next game, Orel heard Tommy yelling, "C'mon Bulldog, you can do it!"

From that point on, Orel began to lose his fear and act like a tenacious fighter. A nickname and a legend were born from that meeting.

↪ Create a Nickname

The possibilities of nicknames are endless: Finding the right one to build a particular trait may take time, but that time spent will pay big dividends. The nickname Stealth gave Lori the confidence she needed to sneak up to the net. Visualizing himself as a bulldog made Orel feel like a fighter on the mound.

As a parent, the key is to help your child find a nickname that brings forth those winning feelings and actions. To accomplish this process, brainstorm together. First, write down five possibilities and the corresponding feelings each inspires.

Nickname	Feelings it promotes
1. _____	_____
2. _____	_____
3. _____	_____
4. _____	_____

5. _____   _____

Next, discuss the benefits and disadvantages of each nickname with your child. Some nicknames will work and some may be problematic. For instance, the nickname Super Glue may be a possibility for a young basketball player who wants to feel like he can stick like glue when playing defense. However, his friends might make fun of this unusual nickname, which could cause problems.

Ask your child for ideas: His imagination, creativity, and self-knowledge may surprise you. A name he thinks of himself will be the most effective.

⇨ Get a Lifeline

A lifeline, a pithy statement of your philosophy, can guide your child's attitude and decisions. The lifeline for John McEnroe, the world-class tennis player, is "Always move forward." John said his desire is to continually move forward in his life. He wants to always learn new things and try to be a better person every day. Besides being a tennis player, John has played the guitar in a band and hosted his own talk show; he currently commentates tennis matches for television.

Help your child create a lifeline. Here are a few examples:

- Trust my skills.
- Always keep learning.
- Never give up and never give in.
- I am the captain of my ship.
- Make sure I'm right, then go ahead.
- Treat myself well.

27

GET YOUR BUTTERFLIES
TO FLY IN FORMATION

Monica came home crying. Continually taunted by a mean girl at school, she was extremely upset. This ridicule had been going on for weeks. At first Monica's mom told her to ignore it, but that did not work. She then recommended that Monica say "whatever" with a sarcastic tone each time the mean girl gave her a verbal jab. But that did not work either.

Monica's mom then told her daughter that they should make up a story about the mean girl. The story started out describing how this mean girl lives with five older sisters who continually taunt her. The mother of the mean girl does not care about her and the father left five years earlier. There is barely enough money for food at their home, and certainly not enough for any new clothes. Monica's mother said, "Now every time this mean girl says anything nasty to you, just remember this story."

The next day at school, the mean girl came up, and as usual, started taunting Monica. But this time, Monica thought about the story and felt a sense of compassion for the mean girl. All the taunts bounced right off, as if she were wearing an emotional suit of armor. The story had made Monica look at this girl in a whole new light. More importantly, the mean girl knew something had changed in their interaction and never bothered Monica again.

Monica's mother used a principle of performance that psychologists have been studying for thirty years: How we interpret a situation will influence how we feel. When Monica looked at the mean girl with compassionate eyes instead of angry eyes, her feelings greatly changed.

Changing the labels we give a situation can radically alter our emotions. Take this example: Your child slams the door on your finger while getting out of the car, but you believe it was accidental. You will probably feel a lot of pain and perhaps a bit of anger. But if you believe your child slammed the door *purposefully* on your finger, your anger will greatly overshadow your pain. By changing your interpretation of the situation, your emotions change.

This performance principle works very well when controlling emotions such as anxiety and feelings of pressure. Successful people label pressure in such a way that it becomes beneficial, and in turn, pressure becomes their friend. The following drills show children how to harness the power of anxiety.

⇨ Channel the Pressure

To a track star, the Olympics are the pinnacle of pressure. And there is no contest in the Olympics more filled with tension than the finals of a track event. But that stress and strain fueled the fire for track star Michael Johnson, and he said, "I crave the pressure. The higher the stakes, the better I am." Michael embraced this pressure and then used it as a catalyst for his incredible speed. He used the power of anxiety to his advantage, an advantage that helped him win a gold medal in both the 100-meter and 200-meter races in the 1996 Olympics.

Extend this example to your children. Most likely, they will feel pressure before taking a test, before going on stage for a recital, and before running on the playing field at the start of a competition. Unfortunately, most children label pressure and anxiety as a negative emotion. They interpret the butterflies and heart palpitations as analogous to the iceberg that destroyed the *Titanic*: They see these nervous feelings as leading to an impending disaster.

As a parent, your goal should be to help your child turn anxiety into a positive energy source. This may be accomplished with a reinterpretation (a relabeling) of the situation, just as Monica's mother did for Monica.

There is an old adage in psychology: "It's okay to have butterflies. Just make sure you get them to fly in formation." Being anxious does not necessarily hurt performance. Actually, anxiety has the potential to increase our capability to accomplish extraordinary feats.

Convince your children that the butterflies are something to embrace as a gift. When we are anxious, our body surges with hormones that promote the accuracy of our eyesight, increase the acuteness of our hearing, and enhance the precision of our touch and feel. These hormones also can intensify our focus as well as quicken our pace on the track.

Here are a few statements that can relabel pressure into a positive force:

- I love this feeling.
- Butterflies can make me fly down the track.
- When I feel like this, I know I am ready.
- I am surging with energy.
- I love this challenge!

Mihaly Csikszentmihalyi, author of the bestselling book *Flow*, emphasizes the importance of relabeling and has said, "Of all the virtues we can learn, no trait is more useful, more essential for survival and more likely to improve the quality of life than the ability to transform adversity into an enjoyable challenge." Convince your children to harness that energy and channel it into something wonderful.

↻ See Anxiety as a Wake-Up Call

Encourage your children to embrace anxiety as a wake-up call. Feeling nervous about not performing well can make us reassess our preparedness for the upcoming event.

Psychologists call this constructive worrying, because it places you on a path of preparedness. When embraced, anxiety can make your child study more and practice more, leading to higher success in any situation.

When your child doesn't feel nervous before an important event, then it is time to worry.

28

Let Go of What Others Think

The human condition is to be concerned about what others think of us. We have a great need to demonstrate our competence, and when we believe our actions or behaviors dictate otherwise, we can get extremely nervous and anxiety-ridden. Albert Einstein called focusing on the affection from others a prison. When we become locked into what others think, we can never achieve our potential.

But this mental prison of human insecurity is nothing new. Aesop wrote about it in one of his fables more than two thousand years ago. In this story a father and son were taking their donkey to town to sell it. Their journey took them through a few neighboring villages. When they arrived at the first village, a group of women laughed at them because they were both walking alongside the donkey instead of riding it. Upon hearing this, the father suggested that his son ride the donkey to town. When they arrived at the next village, one townsperson shouted that the son had no respect for his elders and that the young son should let the old man ride the donkey and rest his weary limbs. Upon hearing this, the father told his son to dismount so he could ride the donkey into town. At the next village, a woman commented that it was shameful for the father to let his young son walk. Not knowing what else to do, the father pulled his son up on the donkey and they rode together. Upon arriving at the next village, they were criticized for overloading the donkey. So they decided to carry the donkey with his feet tied to a pole. While crossing a bridge, the donkey kicked one of his feet loose, causing the son to drop his end of the pole. The donkey fell off the bridge, landed in the river, and drowned. The father realized that when you try to please everyone, you please no one and you can lose your prized possessions in the process.

The pressure of trying to please everyone forced Jennifer Capriati right off the women's tennis tour. In 1991, she was a fourteen-year-old tennis phenom with the spotlight shining brightly on her career, sometimes too brightly. At first, her career took a turn upward, reaching three Grand Slam semifinals and capturing the Olympic gold at Barcelona in 1992. However, she took a sudden nosedive and by the end of the 1993 season, she had left the tour.

Even more dramatic was subsequent news of a drug arrest and a shoplifting incident. She had hit rock bottom.

After a sabbatical of a few years, she returned to women's tennis with a renewed sense of vigor and enthusiasm. She beat Martina Hingis, the world's number one at the time, to win her first ever Grand Slam in Australia.

Jennifer was able to make her dramatic return because she stopped caring about the opinion of others and she learned to stop believing the bad stuff written about her. She ultimately let go of what others thought about her and this gave her peace of mind.

This concern about how others view us is also pervasive in sports other than tennis. Ask Ian Baker-Finch, the winner of the British Open in 1991. Within seven years of his major victory, he had retired from professional golf. Many factors contributed to this decision; one was his humiliating opening round score of 92 at the British Open at Troon and another was his thirty-two straight missed cuts on the tournament trail. However, Ian said what finally caused him to leave the tour was the pressure of what everyone was thinking about his poor performance. He said, "What I would like to be able to do is to change my name, come back in a different body, and go play without the pressure of being Ian Baker-Finch."

Acting is another field where focusing on what others are thinking can kill a career or simply ruin a performance. Laura Linney, who has appeared in many Hollywood blockbusters, says actors can never succeed if they are worried about how others view them—once you get too self-conscious, you are ruined as an actor.

Unfortunately, we are conditioned to focus on what others are thinking of us. The media bombards us with messages that tell us to spend our time and energy on what we are wearing, how we are performing, and who we are impressing.

Fortunately, focusing upon the needs of others can revamp that thinking. It may even jump-start a career: Just ask Carly Simon.

⇨ Focus on the Needs of Others

Given her beautiful voice, it may surprise you to learn that when Carly Simon was growing up, she stuttered. As a young child, she sometimes stammered so severely that she could barely speak in public.

She was so disabled by her fears that she would actually become sick in the morning. Fearing the other students would make fun of her, she dreaded going to school. Her focus upon what others thought of her caused her problems to become even more severe.

Then one morning after a particularly bad patch, her mother said, "If you can start thinking about other people rather than yourself all the time, you may begin to lose your self-consciousness." Her mother believed that she could beat her insecurities when she focused on the needs of other people.

The strategy worked. It transformed her. Carly began to become genuinely interested in others. By focusing on others she not only got rid of her stuttering, she also became the most popular girl in her class.

Is your child self-conscious? Does she focus mainly on what others think of her? Have your child focus on the needs of others in her class or in the community. Ask her questions such as:

- How did you show compassion today?
- How did you help other students in your class today?
- How did you help your community today?

Questioning your child in this regard will help her take the focus off worrying about what others think. Developing a concern for others should free her from the mental prison of pleasing. In that way, she will be able to internalize the moral of Aesop's fable and "ride the donkey" down any path without fear.

GET RATIONAL

Joseph Campbell, who authored many books on cultural myths, told a story in one of his books about a Native American proverb. In this proverb, one elder is giving advice to the boys in the tribe on the day of their initiation into adulthood. The elder tells the boys that as you go your way in this life, you will come to many great chasms. Many of these chasms will seem fraught with danger. But, when you see them, jump—for they are never as wide as you think.

As Campbell found, all cultures have similar beliefs about life. One prevalent theme is that our fears can become exaggerated in our heads. Centuries ago, William Shakespeare acknowledged this theme in *Macbeth* and devised the famous line, "Present fears are less than horrible imaginings." We tend to have irrational fears and irrational beliefs. When these grow out of proportion, our emotional growth will be stunted.

Even great athletes are susceptible to irrational beliefs that can prevent them from playing their best. The all-time great Dodger pitcher Sandy Koufax is one such example. When Sandy first came to the Major Leagues, he believed that he had to throw darts to get the batter out. In other words, he had to throw the ball very precisely, or the batter would get a hit. That, of course, is not true. But that irrational belief regarding precision caused Sandy to feel excessive pressure. Ironically, by trying to get so precise, Sandy was losing his control. This irrational belief was causing a decline in his performance on the mound.

To help Sandy overcome this belief, his catcher, Norm Sherry, explained to him that he could get batters out by widening his target. Rather than use the mitt as the target, Sandy was told to pick up Norm's body as the frame of reference for the pitch. With a wider target, Koufax no longer tried to be a dart thrower. He just let the ball fly, and fly it did. He threw four no-hitters and ended up in the Hall of Fame.

Albert Ellis, one of the foremost psychologists of the twentieth century, understood how irrational beliefs could devastate personal growth. He developed Rational Emotive Behavior Therapy, which works on the concept that many of our anxieties result from irrational beliefs. To reduce our anxiety, we need to change our irrational beliefs into more rational thoughts. When we accomplish this process, we open our channels for human growth.

As in the Native American proverb, your children will come to many chasms in their life. At times, they will wrongly believe that they must turn back, instead of jump.

Parents should teach their children how to recognize these irrational fears as well as how to change them into more realistic thoughts. When this realization occurs, your children will reach their potential. The following drills illustrate some of the principles of Rational Emotive Behavior Therapy so that parents can help their children jump the unrealistic chasms in life.

⟳ Rationalize the Problem

Albert Ellis proposed a list of irrational beliefs that many people have which can cause an increase in anxiety. These include such beliefs as:

- I must be liked by everyone.
- I must appear competent at all times.
- Things must go as planned or it is terrible.
- I must solve all my problems today.
- Success to me is all or nothing.
- Life should be fair.

Your child may have a few of these irrational beliefs, as well as some not on this list, that could be limiting his potential and causing undue stress. To change his irrational beliefs into more rational thoughts, follow a simple three-step procedure.

1. Have your child make a list of worries and thoughts about a given event (such as an upcoming audition, playing on the soccer team, asking someone out on a date).
2. Go through the list and discuss whether these beliefs are grounded in reality. Have him verify whether these beliefs are true or not. Ask him why this belief is true. Ask him to explain with some facts. Sometimes the belief will be true while other times it will be just an irrational fear grounded in myth and illusion. It is important for your son to have that revelation without you telling him.
3. Ask if these beliefs are blocking his performance. Are these beliefs impeding his success? If he discovers that they are causing problems, he is more likely to change.

Here is an example based on the belief: "I must be liked by everyone." Your son may have this irrational fear when he plays baseball. He may feel that if he makes a mistake or a few mistakes, his friends on the team will not like him. (This is a typical belief many boys and girls have who play on teams.)

Ask him if he has made mistakes in the past on the team. His answer will, of course, be yes. Next, ask him if he has lost any friendships because of his mistakes. His answer will most likely be no. Then discuss with him how he has made mistakes in the past without losing friendships. Discuss with him how this pattern should follow for the future: Mistakes in the future should not hurt his friendships, no more than mistakes in the past. Help him also to understand that if he does lose a friend because of a mistake, then this person was not really a friend and, therefore, it was not a loss.

Also, ask him how this belief about being liked by everyone has affected his feelings. He will most likely state that his fear of losing friends because of mistakes increases his feelings of pressure to play well. Suggest that those feelings are hurting his performance. If he changes this unrealistic belief, he should feel less pressure, resulting in better play.

↻ Reject the Fear of Rejection

The fear of rejection is another irrational belief that can block your child's success. We are very protective of our ego (self-esteem) and so we dislike rejection (a blow to our ego). We will do what it takes to avoid rejection and protect our ego. But in most cases, the rejection is not nearly as bad as we make it out to be: This fear becomes exaggerated in our head, more horrible in the mind than in reality.

To help your child overcome her fear of rejection, explain some of your past rejections to her. Be honest. Let her know how you felt about those rejections. Also, let her know what you learned from your rejections. Another method to get over rejection is to get rejected a few times. Once that happens, your child will see that rejection is not so terrible. Create some rejection opportunities for your child. (Sounds interesting, doesn't it?) For instance, suggest applying for a job. Let's assume your daughter is fourteen and will most likely not get the job due to her age. Also, pick a job that she might not want very badly. After this rejection (if it does happen), discuss her feelings about the rejection and illustrate that rejection itself was not such a terrible happening.

Another technique to help your daughter get over rejection is to implement "the worst case scenario" technique. For instance, suppose your daughter is in the orchestra on stage, playing a piece of music. What is the worst case scenario? She missed a few notes during the piece. Explain to her that such an event would not be catastrophic. She would just continue to play and most people would not notice her mistake.

Or suppose your son plays goalie on his soccer team. What is the worst case scenario? Perhaps the opposing team scores four goals. Is that really terrible? Explain that many professional goalies allow more goals than that every game. Further, point out that there is always next week to prevent goals.

Or suppose your daughter asks a boy to the school dance. What is the worst case scenario? He says no. That is it. Of course that may hurt, but as they say, "There are many fish in the sea."

⇨ Let Go of the Perfection Syndrome

Carl Jung, the famous mid-twentieth-century psychologist, once lamented, "Perfection belongs to the gods; the most that we can hope for is excellence." Carl Jung is right. Being perfect is impossible. Believing we should be perfect is irrational. More importantly, striving for perfection causes undue pressure. Teach your child to de-emphasize perfection at all costs. It is irrational for your son to believe he has to get all the answers correct on every test. Your daughter will get stressed out if she believes that her outfit has to be perfect. Your son will most likely feel high anxiety if he believes he cannot make any mistakes or hit any bad shots on the golf course.

Teach your children to strive for excellence. Perfection, in most cases, is not humanly possible.

30

CREATE POSITIVE
SUPERSTITIONS

Superstitions are rampant in all walks of life. Many people avoid the number thirteen. Others do not walk under ladders or try not to break any mirrors. Some of us avoid stepping on cracks and crossing the path of a black cat. We believe violating these superstitions will give us bad luck.

Sports has its share of superstitious behavior. Take Chi-Chi Rodriguez, the golfing star from Puerto Rico, as a prime example of a superstitious soul. During any given round he carried a lucky rock. He always marked his ball with the head side up. When he had a birdie putt, he marked the ball with a quarter. If he had a good round, he would take the same route to and from the golf course.

Ben Crenshaw is another golfer who enjoys his superstitions. He only plays with low-numbered balls, one through four. He does not want to make a score higher than what is marked on the ball, so he prefers not to use any large numbers on his golf balls.

In tennis, Bjorn Borg never shaved during his Wimbledon days. Ken Flach, doubles winner at Wimbledon and the U.S. Open, had a unique after-point ritual: He only walked in the doubles alley when the point was over; he never walked the tee of the tennis court.

Wade Boggs, the Hall of Fame baseball player, had his famous chicken superstition: He liked to eat a chicken dinner before he played his baseball games. David Toms also believed in the "power of chicken." He was not playing well coming into the 2001 PGA championship. He ate a chicken dinner from Chick-fil-A before the round and played really well the next day. So, he continued eating Chick-fil-A chicken before each round and won his first major championship that week.

Writers of great literature have their superstitions as well. Charles Dickens, author of *A Christmas Carol,* believed that when he faced due north his energy levels for writing were increased. Gertrude Stein enjoyed writing while waiting at railroad crossings. She believed that train noise helped her tap into her creative thoughts.

In addition, the arts are colored with unique behaviors. Andrew, a young concert violinist, taps on his case three times before opening it the day of his recitals. Samantha, an artist, never uses the color "passion purple," believing that this color has negative undertones—she does not want to risk giving her audience a bad impression of her painting.

While these behaviors may seem strange, they provide a purpose. Life is very unpredictable. Wanting control over our world is human nature. Superstitions provide us with a perceived sense of control. By engaging in the action, we believe we have greater influence over the outcome. That is, if Chi-Chi marks his ball with a quarter rather than a nickel, he believes the putt will more likely fall because of his action. If we do not walk under ladders, we believe our days will be filled with great tidings.

Are superstitions good for us?

The perceived sense of control derived from our superstitions can give us peace of mind and a more relaxed attitude. We believe we will perform better if we engage in these superstitions, which removes some of the pressure we feel. In actuality, if we are more relaxed, we probably will perform better.

Do your children engage in superstitious thoughts or behavior before their performance?

Some superstitions can be positive while some can become counterproductive to your child's achievement. The following drills will help your child avoid negative superstitions while creating positive ones.

↻ Avoid Negative Superstitions

Some superstitions can reduce our chances of performing well. For instance, one morning your daughter skipped breakfast and afterward, she played her best tennis match ever. Now she sticks with that behavior and skips breakfast before all her matches. She believes breakfast adds weight and slows her down. However, it is a bad nutritional choice to neglect the most important meal of the day.

Another problem can occur when a player has a sinking feeling because she did not get to engage in her superstitious behavior before the event. Let's say that your daughter has the ritual of wearing a wristband when she plays basketball. But on the day of a big game, she loses her favorite wristband and believes she will play terribly without it. Of course, the wristband does not influence her play, but if she believes it does, then its absence is likely to affect her performance.

To avoid any possible complications with negative superstitions, ask your daughter to list all her rituals before play. Analyze the list together. Discuss with her the faulty rationality behind negative superstitions and why they can be problematic.

⊙ Create Positive Superstitions

Why not help your son develop "superstitions" that promote better play?

Joey Sindelar, a PGA pro, starts every par five with a new ball. A golf ball can get out of round very easily, thus this belief will provide a greater chance for better scores.

Here is a list of positive superstitious habits that can add to your child's good play:

- Wearing two socks on each foot—this gives greater cushion to his joints.
- Sharpening his pencil before every test—this promotes clearer writing for the teacher to grade.
- Cleaning her instrument before every recital—a shiny instrument can help to influence the judges.
- Eating a nutritious breakfast before every test or competition—breakfast helps kick-start the mind and body into motion.

Help your child develop positive habits that not only increase his good luck but also add to his great play.

31

INOCULATE YOURSELF AGAINST CHOKING

I play this piece so well at home," Grant said to his orchestra teacher. "But every time I play it for you or for the class, I mess up." Befuddled, Grant added, "I just don't get why I choke in front of you and my friends."

"Consequences," Grant's teacher said. "You practice without consequences and then when the pressure is on, when you have consequences, it is a different animal, and you goof up. You need to practice with consequences. You need to put pressure on yourself in practice. For example, when you are practicing a piece at home, have a rule that for every mistake you make, you must give your little brother a nickel. Your little brother may get richer, but his new wealth will get you mentally ready for the upcoming recital."

The Flying Wallendas know the importance of consequences and they live by that principle in their practice routines. This group of trapeze artists performs without a net. They have performed some of their most dangerous stunts two hundred feet in the air without a net. This performance routine is what has made them famous.

What most people do not know about the Flying Wallendas is that they practice without a net as well. They understand the principle of practicing with consequences. If they practiced with a net and then the net was taken away during their show, they might get more nervous and perform poorly, possibly falling to their death. Practicing without a net and then performing without a net ensures that nothing is changed: These performers are as focused in practice as they are during a performance.

To perform at their best under pressure, the Wallendas use the principle of situational similarity. Performance psychologists have long known that the best way to prevent choking under pressure is to create practice situations as similar as possible to performance situations. In essence, when the practice situations mimic pressure conditions, individuals will have a greater transfer of skills to the performance realm.

Parents who help create pressure situations in practice can help their children to feel more at peace in the competitive world. Preparing your children to be comfortable in the uncomfortable is a key to helping them play their best under pressure. The following drills will help inoculate your children against choking.

⟳ Practice Your Reality

To inoculate your children against choking, it would help if they understand how to react when the pressure is on. To accomplish this, they need to place pressure on themselves during practice. Perhaps the greatest clutch kicker in NFL history, Adam Vinatieri applies the pressure when he practices. During practice, he always kicks with his helmet on and buckled. He gets team officials to pipe in crowd noise during practice. Adam times every kick he makes in practice, from when the ball is snapped to the time he kicks it, making sure nothing changes from practice to the real game. Perhaps these practice principles have helped his teams win two Super Bowls with his last-second kicks.

When you are helping your child get ready for a test, have him take a mock exam. Many books have practice exams at the end of the chapters. Have your son do that exam, but time it just like the real test. If your child gets forty-five minutes to complete the upcoming test, make sure he gets that same time on the mock test. Further, if your child does not get a certain number correct, create an agreement where he has to study twice as long the following night. Now that is a consequence!

⟳ Inoculate Yourself against Choking

Phil Mickelson, the great golfer, has a putting drill where he sets a series of golf balls about three feet from the cup. He has to make 100 in succession.

If he misses one, he has to start over. When he gets to ninety, you had better believe that Phil is feeling the pressure. But more importantly, he is learning how to react to pressure under the ease of a practice session.

Conduct a similar drill with your child. If he plays basketball, you should instruct him to make a certain number in a row from the free throw line (such as ten in a row), and if he misses one, have the count start all over. When the eighth and ninth free throws come around, he likely will be feeling the pressure as in a real game.

○ Make Practice Your Masterpiece

Michael Jordan made practice his masterpiece. According to Ed Nealy, Michael's former teammate, Michael took practicing to a new level. Ed said, "They should have charged admission for every Bulls' practice because you would have seen more from Michael there than in the games. It didn't matter if we'd played five games in eight days. MJ would practice like it was his last day in uniform."

Michael knew the harder he played in practice, the easier it would be for him to get "comfortable in the uncomfortable." He respected practice because he knew that these sessions could take him to the next level, if taken seriously. The more pressure he put on himself in practice, the easier it was for him to respond effectively under the gun of the real game.

Encourage your children to treat practice as seriously as it should be. Teach them to treat practice with respect, as Michael and Phil did, and chances are much greater that their opponents will respect them for it, before, during, and after the competition.

32

KICK THE ANXIETY HABIT

Sarah is frustrated and very upset. She failed geometry last semester, but this year she has a new teacher. Sarah really likes her new teacher and believes this new teacher makes the material easy to understand. But during the last test Sarah completely blanked out—she forgot practically everything she had studied, and she studied a lot.

Like millions of other students, Sarah has test anxiety, and in her case, it is quite severe. When students have test anxiety, their brains release hormones that can block their ability to remember, and thus, students "blank out" during tests.

One of the major problems with test anxiety is that we can condition our brains to have it. Regardless of whether Sarah is confident, or whether she studied a lot or likes the teacher, she may still get test anxiety in geometry class.

This same conditioning principle can happen to elite athletes as well. They can condition themselves to get nervous before a match, regardless of how confident or competent they are in their sport. It happened to Bill Russell.

Bill Russell, Hall of Famer for the Boston Celtics, is known as the best team basketball player of all time. He won more championships than any other player. In his autobiography, *Russell Rules*, Bill said he always believed in his abilities and loved to play the game. Yet before most games, he would throw up. This act became a habit. Bill had conditioned his body to be extremely nervous before every game he played, regardless of his enjoyment of the game or his confidence level.

Analyzing the principles of classical conditioning can help us understand how Sarah and Bill trained their bodies to have performance anxiety. Classical conditioning was discovered almost a hundred years ago by the Russian scientist Ivan Pavlov. In his famous experiment with dogs, he paired the ringing of a bell with the presentation of food. After a number of pairings with the bell, Pavlov found that if he removed the food, the ringing of the bell alone would produce saliva in the mouths of dogs.

Like the dogs in Pavlov's experiment, we get conditioned when we continually pair our bodies with certain responses. For Sarah, in the previous year, she continually paired taking geometry tests with the feeling of being nervous. In this new year, she has geometry test anxiety regardless of how much she studies. When Bill Russell was younger, he felt nervous before basketball games. He trained his body to be nervous. As he got older, those feelings of nervousness did not subside.

The good news is that we can unlearn these conditioned responses. With the appropriate techniques, parents can help their children reduce test anxiety as well as performance anxiety in sports and other venues. The following drills should help your children recondition their nervous feelings into more effective responses.

⇨ Recondition Your Body

One of the best methods to help your child recondition her body is with the educational technique called systematic desensitization (SD). This is a fancy name for a simple technique in which you visualize anxiety-provoking images while you are relaxed. The underlying principle is that the relaxation response is stronger than the anxiety response. When you pair those two responses together, the relaxation response wins out and the anxiety will be reduced.

SD can work to reduce test anxiety in three easy steps. First, have your child create a sequential list of actions leading up to the test. The list should go from images that are least anxiety-producing to most anxiety-producing, with the most stressful being the actual taking of the test. Here is an example of a sequential list that could be used for your child:

1. She enters the school grounds.
2. She walks over to the classroom where the test will be taken.
3. She walks into the classroom.
4. She sits down at her desk.
5. She watches the teacher distribute the test.
6. She receives the test.
7. She begins to take the test.

In the second step, your child should get relaxed. Use the procedure described in the Find a Calm Spot drill on page 40.

Once your child has achieved a relaxed state, the last step is to have her visualize each action in order, starting with arriving on the school grounds and finishing with taking the test.

But do not stop with test taking. Suggest to your daughter that she apply SD to any and all situations that cause her anxiety, from speaking in front of groups to music recitals.

PART 5

EMOTIONAL DRIVE: POWER ON

To become a champion in any field, knowledge is not enough. Intention is not enough. To get results, action is essential. But action takes motivation and high levels of energy.

Winners have emotional drive. They power on, regardless of the situation or outcome. People like Arnold Schwarzenegger, Bill Bradley, and Angelina Jolie are committed to their cause. They know what it takes to fulfill their destiny and achieve excellence and are willing to put forth the energy needed.

Is your child committed to excellence? Does your child put forth the effort needed to be a winner and achieve her potential?

This section focuses on creating boundless energy and commitment to the cause of excellence. You will discover how your children can develop drive and adhere to a plan of action, both of which are essential to becoming a winner in life.

33

WORK YOUR WAY
TO EXCELLENCE

While walking down the street in Paris one lovely afternoon, Pablo Picasso was approached by an admirer. After introducing herself and praising his work, she asked him if he would consider drawing her portrait. She offered to pay him and Picasso agreed. He got out his sketchbook and pencil and began to draw, right there on the side of the street. He finished the drawing in just a few minutes and handed it to the woman. He told her it would be 5,000 francs, a handsome sum in those days. Surprised at the price, the woman objected and said that the portrait had only taken a few minutes to complete.

Picasso smiled and replied, "No, my dear woman, you are mistaken; it took me a whole lifetime."

Most of us do not see all the hard work it takes to master an art, sport, or musical instrument. We never see the journey—we only see the endpoint of all the hard work. The famous musician Vladimir Horowitz once said, "If I don't practice for one day, I will know it. If I do not practice for two days, my wife knows it. If I don't practice for three days, the world knows it." Every great success story has one facet in common— hard work.

One of the greatest success stories of our generation, and perhaps of all time, is that of Arnold Schwarzenegger. He came to this country from Austria and began work as a bricklayer. At that time, he also was working on his fabulous physique. He eventually dominated bodybuilding with seven Mr. Olympia titles, the sport's highest honor. These honors helped catapult him into the movie industry, where he struggled with the English language. However, he persevered and rose to become a movie star. But his success did not stop there. As we know, he became governor of the state of California. Who knows how far he will go in the field of politics?

Arnold said he followed three main directives to achieve his great successes: Be confident, have a positive outlook, and work as hard as you can. Arnold further added that most people believe they work hard, but, in actuality, they do not put forth the effort necessary to succeed. To him, the road to success is paved with hard work.

Tom Hanks, another famous actor, delivered a very poignant line about work in the movie *A League of Their Own*, in which he played the manager of a women's professional baseball team. In one pep talk to his team after a few losses, Tom's character epitomizes the importance of hard work by shouting, "The hard is what makes it great!"

It can be quite a challenge to convince children that they must work extremely hard if they want to achieve success. Convincing them that "the hard is what makes it great" may seem impossible. But getting your children to work hard in life is extremely important, if not essential. Nothing is given freely in this world. The following are suggestions to parents about how to illustrate to children that hard work is essential.

↻ Have a Catchphrase

Jim Courier, a winner of twenty-three singles titles and former number one tennis player in the world, had a catchphrase when he was slacking in his work ethic. Actually, his dad developed the catchphrase. When Jim was not giving his full effort, whether it was in academics or sports, his dad would say, "There are a lot of talented people in the unemployment line." This always reminded Jim that talent would only take him so far. If he wanted to be successful, he had better start working harder.

Develop a catchphrase like Jim. Here are a few examples:

- The road to success is paved with hard work.
- The ingredients for success are talent and hard work.
- No one was ever born with a great forehand (golf swing, free throw shot, etc.).

Make sure this phrase reminds your child that talent is not enough. Hard work is essential.

↻ Invest in Your Work Ethic

If your child likes math, counting, or making money, then the following analogy about hard work will be potent.

Work is an investment. Like depositing money, you put work into the "work bank." You have to let it accrue for a while. Then after a given time, you will see your investment shine. But you must be patient about your investment.

This philosophy of making deposits to the work bank helped Bjorn Borg achieve his greatness on the tennis court. Bjorn remembers taking the train every day after school to play tennis, eventually arriving home late, studying, waking up early the next morning to go to school, and then getting on the train again to head back to the courts. This routine continued for many years. It took a lot of effort, but the investment paid off in the end because he gave tennis his best shot.

Have your child invest in his best and the dividends will astound him.

↻ Get Lucky with Hard Work

Most people believe that luck contributes to success. Children may also believe that luck plays a part in their success, whether on the playing field or in the classroom. But as the old saying goes, luck happens when opportunity meets preparation. The harder your children work, the more prepared they will be. There will always be opportunities that arise for your children. If they want to make their own luck, your children must be well prepared when any possibility arises.

↻ Work Harder than the Next Person

In all likelihood, at some point in your child's life, there will be someone gunning for his job or position. Whether it is playing first string on the football team or being the first violinist in the orchestra, he needs to remember that someone is in line for his position.

How then can he keep his position?

Work harder than the next person. That was always the life philosophy of all-time great Bill Bradley, former professional basketball star as well as a U.S. Senator. He said he learned this life lesson from one of his favorite coaches who told him, "When you are not practicing, someone else is, and given equal ability, when you meet, he will win."

Bill did not like to lose, so he gave maximum effort. From June to September, four days a week, three hours a day, he ran along the streets. To improve his vertical leap, he wore weights in his shoes, and he jumped to touch the rim—eighty times a day. To practice dribbling, he wore plastic glasses that prevented him from looking down at the ball, which forced him to keep his eyes on the court.

Bill said his work ethic carried over to many other areas of his life, from academics (he was a Rhodes Scholar) to politics. Bill still believes that no one can outwork him.

Encourage your child to follow this same philosophy. If your child does not have a spot on the team or position in the orchestra yet, suggest that he work harder than the next person. If he already has a spot on the team or position in the orchestra, suggest that he work harder than the next person. In either regard, your child should follow the philosophy of the African parable that says:

> Every morning in Africa, the gazelle wakes up and knows it must run faster than the fastest lion.
> Every morning, a lion wakes up and knows it must outrun the slowest gazelle or it will starve.
> It does not matter whether you are a gazelle or a lion,
> When the sun comes up, you better start running.

⟳ Excellence Has Its Price

More than two thousand years ago, the Greek philosopher Epictetus remarked, "Those who win at something have no real advantage over you because they had to pay the price for the reward." Times have not changed: To be successful, it takes not only hard work but also great sacrifice.

Make sure your children know that excellence takes time and toil. We typically only see the end point in the journey to excellence, not its trials and tribulations. We rarely see the inner workings of mastering a task—how the long hours of practice take away time from friends and leisure. Help your children appreciate that the attainment of expertise does not come cheaply.

34

Enjoy Every Interaction

As a young rising star in China, Ming Lee travels her country from one concert hall to the next, impressing audiences wherever she plays. Still only fourteen years of age, she has mastered the great composers, from Chopin to Tchaikovsky. One night on her tour at the Chin Concert Hall in the providence of Yandang Shan, Ming's music seemed stifled and lacking in passion.

At the end of the concert, her mother, who is her teacher and a former concert pianist, asked her daughter what happened on stage that night. Ming responded bitterly, "This hall is old and the music does not resonate. With all its nooks and crannies, the sound just bounces across the stage." While her mother knew the hall lacked the acoustical refinements of newer ones, she responded, "You do not like this hall, so it does not like you. Rejoice in its uniqueness and your music will sing."

We can talk ourselves into performing well as easily as we can talk ourselves into performing poorly. If we believe that this particular concert hall has fantastic acoustics, then we will be more likely to perform beautifully. But if we despise the place, our performance may suffer. For Ming, when she learns to love Chin Hall, her music will begin to love her.

Brad Gilbert exemplifies this same principle in the sport of tennis. Brad knew the importance of loving every tennis venue. Brad, author of the book *Winning Ugly*, did indeed look ugly on the court: He did not play with the grace and grandeur of the other top ranked tennis players. It was not pretty to watch him hit a forehand, to say the least. But Brad had a knack for beating the best pros in the game, even when they seemed to have the better game. In fact, he was known as the giant killer in his playing days for beating all the top ranked pros. Brad mastered his ability to talk himself into winning tennis matches. He just knew how to win ugly.

A perfect example of winning ugly occurred between Brad Gilbert and Boris Becker at the 1987 U.S. Open. Any expert would have told you that Boris, with all his talent, would beat Brad. Boris was an all-time great, with three Wimbledon titles under his belt. But this was the U.S. Open at Flushing Meadows in September, with many distractions to throw a game into disarray. The weather was hot and muggy, planes were continually flying overhead, and the crowd was very rowdy.

Becker won the first two sets (6-2, 7-6) and was leading 3-0 in the third. Then the rain came, and the momentum turned. After the rain delay, Brad came back and broke Boris's serve. Fans began to roll in from other matches. The crowd got behind Brad and they began to chant "U-S-A." Boris lost the third set in a tiebreaker and proceeded to lose the next two sets, and subsequently the match.

Later that night, after the match, Brad and Boris ran into each other at a local restaurant. Boris began to complain to Brad about all the distractions at the U.S. Open. Boris went on to mention that it had been too hot and that the crowd had turned hostile toward him. Brad, on the other hand, responded that he loved all those distractions. He declared that he loved the U.S. Open because it is such a wild circus and such an exciting venue. In effect, Boris had talked himself out of winning while Brad won because he loved the chaos at the Open.

It is really that simple. Children can convince themselves that they do really enjoy every golf course or tennis court or concert hall, and chances are they will perform at higher levels. Parents should encourage their children to fall in love with every venue. But this performance principle goes much deeper than just venues. Children also should enjoy every interaction they have, from competition with certain opponents to interactions with friends or teachers. When they make every interaction their favorite, children will thrive in the world. The following drills can help parents guide their children into believing that every interaction is a favorite.

⇨ Make Every Teacher Your Favorite

Not every teacher will be competent, or your daughter's favorite. That is a given. When your daughter does not like a teacher, for whatever reason, her grades may suffer as a result. She may tune out the teacher or just not try as hard because of her distaste for the teacher.

To resolve this difficulty, find out which teachers your daughter likes and which ones she does not. Ask her to tell you what some of the differences are between her favorite and least favorite teachers. This discussion will help you understand the factors that lead her to dislike some of her teachers.

For the teachers she dislikes, discuss how she can focus on some qualities that could have positive aspects.

Perhaps the disliked teacher is too tough. If so, discuss with your daughter how the teacher's toughness can make her a better student as well as a smarter person.

Perhaps the teacher goes off on a tangent when speaking about a particular topic. Discuss with your daughter how she could enjoy those entertaining and interesting stories about life.

⇨ Make Every Topic Your Favorite

There will be some topics at school that your daughter readily enjoys and some topics she would rather not study. This disinterest can lead to poorer grades. Most likely, the more your child enjoys the topic of study, the better her grades.

Usually, there are always some parts of a topic that have some attraction. For instance, let's say your daughter dislikes math. But she may like to draw and create. Illustrate how certain aspects of math (such as geometry) can relate to being creative. Once you open the door with one aspect of math, try another, and then another.

⇨ Make Every Opponent Your Favorite

Some opponents do not match up well with your son or his team. For instance, if he is a tennis player, aggressive players may not match up well with his offensive style. Most likely, those are the opponents your son will not like to play. On the other hand, your son loves to play defensive style players and he usually beats those types like a drum. Convince him that there will be some aspects of an opponent's game (or team) that match up well with his game. Encourage him to focus on those key characteristics. When he starts winning, he will like those opponents that much more.

◇ Make Every Course Your Friend

Jack Nicklaus loves Augusta National, the venue where the Masters golf tournament is played. He said that he still gets goose bumps when he rides up Magnolia Lane, the entrance to Augusta National.

Lee Trevino, another all-time great, has said that he does not like Augusta National. He has commented that it is not a great golf course and that the course does not fit his game. Jack has won the Masters six times; Lee has never won a Masters, though he has won every other major. Perhaps if Lee felt the love for Augusta that Jack does, Lee may have won there.

There are many reasons why certain players perform better on certain golf courses. One factor is that a course may fit a player's eye. The holes just seem to line up well for a particular player. As a result of this perception, shots set up well throughout the course. Similarly, a course may be a predominately left-to-right shot course, and certain players favor that shot pattern.

Most likely, however, it is this simple reason: Players just like some courses more than others, and they talk themselves into playing better on their favorite courses.

Encourage your son to like every course he plays, regardless of whether the course fits his eye or not. In reality, every course will fit his eye if he believes it.

In addition, if your son plays soccer, have him make friends with every field. Have him find positives about every field that match up with his style of play. The same applies to baseball, football, or any sport. The more he loves the venue, the more the venue will love him. It is that simple.

35

SHARE YOUR MEANING

A ngelina Jolie was a wild child. Growing up in Hollywood, she behaved outrageously, engaging in many self-destructive behaviors. She believed she would die young.

As she got older, she followed in her father's footsteps, making movies, but still her success did not change her attitude about life. While she attained financial success and even love, she still believed she had an emptiness inside.

Reading the script for *Beyond Borders* transformed Angelina into a person of purpose. It is a story of a woman who discovers orphans around the world. From that moment, she realized what the meaning of her life was. To date, Angelina has given her time and money to help orphans around the world. She keeps it in perspective and said that making movies and getting awards does not compare in meaning to building schools for needy children.

Angelina changed because now she feels that she is part of the world. Instead of taking, she is giving, creating a meaningful difference in the lives of others.

Finding meaning guides your life like a lighthouse directing a lost boat through the mist. For Angelina, meaning created a beacon to an undeniable path. It gave her intense pleasure, as well as the motivation to make a difference. Her life changed for the better. As John Gardner said a long time ago, "Astonishing sources of energy seem available to those who find meaning in what they are doing."

Besides filling you with boundless energy, meaning can drive away pressure. Tiger Woods's late father, Earl Woods, said that Tiger is bulletproof to the pressure because of the meaning in his life. At the start of his professional career, Tiger started his foundation to help underprivileged children throughout the country. In 2005, the first Tiger Woods center was opened in Los Angeles, where children learn about art, physics, math, and yes, some golf is thrown into the mix.

Earl Woods wrote in *Playing Through* that Tiger plays for much more than just trophies and titles. He is now playing for the kids as well as his foundation, which helps to alleviate the pressure he may feel during tournament play.

Parents want their children to have meaning in their lives. Helping their children discover a meaningful path, however, is one of the most difficult tasks a parent can undertake. The following drill can help children find meaning in their lives.

○ Find Meaning

To help your child discover meaning in his life, ask him to write down five meaningful aspects for each activity in which he participates. For instance, if he plays the viola, then discuss the meaningfulness of this activity. Here are a few examples:

1. I enjoy playing music and hearing the melodies of the song.
2. I give pleasure to the audience.
3. I give pleasure to my parents.
4. My performance helps the orchestra.
5. I can give charity concerts in the future.

For a sport like soccer, his list might include these examples:

1. I enjoy the pure pleasure of kicking the right shot at the right time.
2. I help make the coach happy when I play my best.
3. I help the other players on my team.
4. Playing soccer can help me get a scholarship.
5. I am a good role model for my younger siblings.

Have your son post this list on his door or on his computer. Suggest that he look at this list before a competition, when his nerves are raw, or when he needs a jolt of energy. In either case, his performance will benefit.

36

GET A MENTOR

George Gershwin, the famous composer in the early 1900s, was a great admirer of Ravel, another composer who lived in Paris. Gershwin wrote to Ravel to inquire about studying with him. Ravel did not reply to his letter. Gershwin wrote again and again. Ravel still did not respond to his letter. Being passionate about his quest, Gershwin wrote a fourth time.

Finally, Ravel wrote back and asked Gershwin how he could afford a six-month visit to Paris to study without being employed. George wrote back that he was a very successful composer in New York making almost $100,000 a year, which was a lot of money in those days. He explained that he indeed could afford taking six months off to study with him.

Ravel, in return, responded, "Stay there; I am coming to New York."

Kidding aside, we all need someone to mentor us. Even the all-time greats have had mentors: Take Sir Isaac Newton.

Newton once said that he could see farther by standing on the shoulders of giants. One of those sets of shoulders belonged to Edmond Halley. Most people link the name of Halley to the namesake comet that he discovered. Few know that he mentored Isaac Newton, helping him to become one of the greatest scientists of all time. Halley challenged Newton to think through his original notions and to use mathematics and geometrical figures to clarify his ideas. Furthermore, he encouraged Newton to write his great work *Mathematical Principles of Natural Philosophy*, which Newton had been hesitant to write. Halley also edited the work and supervised its publication. Without the mentoring of Halley, Newton might have only been a footnote in time and space.

Today, mentoring comes in the form of a coach or a teacher. Having the right coach can pay dividends when developing talent. The very successful adult usually had the right coaching at the right time.

In his book *Discovering Talent*, Gordon Bloom investigated young talent from all walks of achievement including the arts, sports, and education. Interestingly, Bloom discovered an important common factor that contributed to their greatness. These talented young people had mentors or coaches that followed a pattern. First, they had a local mentor or coach who first gave them the knowledge base and taught them the basic skills. Next, they were mentored by a "regionally known" coach. This mentor fine-tuned their skills. Finally, they moved to a world-renowned coach, who took them to the next level.

Tim Daggett, the 1984 gold medalist in gymnastics, followed this exact pattern of mentorship. Tim's first mentor was his high school coach, who taught him the basics of his sport. This coach also explained the importance of working out in the off-season. Next, Tim went to UCLA and met a man named Makoto Sakamoto, who became his second mentor. He taught Tim the essentials of training, such as the value of hard work and the necessity of goal-setting. His third mentor was Yefim Furman, a former Soviet gymnast. Furman gave him the technical expertise he needed to reach the top of his sport.

Whether it is Tim or your child, finding the right mentor is essential to developing talent. Here are a few suggestions for selecting the best mentor for your child.

↻ Do Not Rush the Mentoring Process

Mentors must be right for each student's emotional and physical development. It is also important to have a trusting relationship with someone who fits that developmental time frame for your child.

In the beginning of a mentor relationship, parents should give a local coach enough time to develop a child's talent. Do not rush into any coaching changes before your child is ready to move up the coaching ladder.

Unfortunately, some parents rush this process and send their child to a world-renowned coach when it is not necessary. Not only may this be a waste of money, but it may also be a bad match for your child. The famous coach may be all business and this type of seriousness may not be appropriate for your child. At an early stage in your child's "career," fun can be the driving force behind the game, not the competition.

⇨ Know What Makes a Great Mentor

Not all mentors or coaches have been great players or extremely successful in their respective fields. But a competent mentor will be someone who has gained a certain amount of expertise in her field. If the mentor is a music teacher, this person should have played in the local orchestra or had some similar level of experience. If the mentor is a baseball coach, this person should have played college or at least high school baseball. Professional levels are not needed.

And just because someone made it to the professional level does not make this person a great mentor. In fact, such a high level of expertise may be detrimental to coaching. Persons who make it to the professional ranks have a lot of innate ability and sometimes cannot relate to someone who needs to practice many hours to improve.

⇨ Benefit from Being a Mentor

Many schools have both disabled and non-disabled children in the same classrooms. However, meeting all the needs of the children can take a lot of time and energy. In many classes, teachers will ask non-disabled students to help mentor the disabled students; this is known as peer tutoring.

Peer tutoring benefits both students. The disabled student gets to interact with non-disabled students, learning both social and emotional differences. The mentor also benefits, however. Researchers have found that being a mentor increases the mentor's grades as well as decreases his absenteeism. Ultimately, being a mentor makes you a better student.

Ask your child if there are any opportunities to mentor other students in his school. Most likely there will be. Not only will it benefit your child scholastically, but he will also be rewarded in ways that go far beyond the classroom.

37

Map Out Your Dreams

"Jimmy, you need to clean up your room," his mother said. "Your cousins are coming this weekend and they need to share your room." But Jimmy was stumped. It was such a mess, he did not know where to start. He was overwhelmed and just sat in the middle of his room.

Seeing the problem and thinking fast, Jimmy's mother said, "Okay, I'll tell you what we'll do. Let's clean your closet today. We will tackle your computer area and the mess on the floor tomorrow and finish the job on Friday by cleaning your desk area."

Jimmy's mother knew that cleaning the whole room at one time was too daunting of a task for her son. She had to break it into reasonable areas for her son to clean.

To achieve their goals, many athletes use the same principle as Jimmy's mother: They break down their goals into smaller steps. Reaching a goal takes time. It takes small steps—it takes one shot at a time. Or in Robert Gentry's case, one lap at a time.

Robert was vying to win the NCAA championships in the 10,000 meter run. However, Robert believed that to accomplish this, he would have to shave two minutes from his time by next season. Reducing his time by that amount was a daunting task. However, to make this goal attainable, Robert came up with the strategy of increasing his effort on each lap. Robert equated the effort he needed to the snap of his fingers. (To Robert, one snap was equivalent to a 1 percent increase of effort.) Robert believed that if he increased his effort by the equivalent of one snap on each lap, he could decrease his time by one minute. If he increased his effort by the equivalent of two snaps, he could decrease his time by two minutes for the entire race.

Robert made his goals workable: Anyone could increase effort by one or two snaps a lap, or at least Robert believed he could do it. His strategy worked. He decreased his time and became a college star in the 10,000 meters.

When we speak of goals and dreams, we can make an analogy to a staircase. Your ultimate goal is to get to the top of the staircase. Most of us can reach our goals if we know what steps to take and focus on one step at a time, or in Robert's case, one snap at a time.

Your children will have many goals they want to attain in their lives. Most will be reachable, particularly if there is a step-by-step process to attain those goals. The following are guidelines for setting up an effective goal program with your children.

↻ Be Specific

Instead of your child having a general goal for improving her basketball skills or her reading skills, make this goal specific. For instance, an effective goal would be to improve her free throw percentage by 10 percent or increase her reading speed by 10 words a minute. When goals are specific, then they can be measured, which is discussed in the next drill.

↻ Be Measurable

An effective goal-setting program has measurable goals. Everything can be measured. Even psychological goals such as concentration can be measured.

To measure concentration, first have your child create a ranking scale for concentration in 10 point increments with 100 being the best and 0 being the worst. Allow him to label the scale. For instance, 30 equates to "somewhat distracted" while 70 equates to "somewhat focused." The score of 100 equals being "totally focused."

Next, have your child rank his concentration in class or on the playing field. Take about five different assessments and get an average. Let's say your son found out that his concentration in a typical class was 50. Then together, you could set a goal to increase his concentration to 55 for the next month. Setting attainable goals is the next step in the process.

⇨ Set Attainable Goals

Once you have discovered a baseline for a given measure, your goal of improvement should be approximately 10 percent each month. For instance, if your son's reading speed is 40 words a minute, then this month's goal should be to improve that speed to 44 words a minute.

⇨ Create Strategies

Once attainable goals are set, a parent should sit down with the child and develop strategies to reach those goals. For instance, if the goal is to improve basketball free throw percentage by 15 percent, then a strategy could be to shoot free throws for thirty minutes each day.

If your child has a goal to improve his reading speed by 4 words per minute, then a strategy could be to read one book a week. If the goal is to become first string in the violin section of the orchestra, one strategy might be to take lessons from a new instructor.

⇨ Assess the Goals

Once you have goals and strategies, assessment is next. Assess your child's performance every week or at least every two weeks. If your child did not reach the goal of 44 words per minute in reading speed by the end of the first month, then you may want to change his strategy. Instead of reading one book per week, your child may need to read two books per week. Obtaining a tutor is another option.

Once you have an effective goal-setting plan in place for your child, anything is possible.

38

LEAP OVER YOUR PLATEAUS

Jason was known as the next Bobby Fischer, the famed chess master. He started playing chess at the age of four and became the talk of his chess club. He started beating adults by the age of eight, and he attained a chess ranking of 1,200 by the age of ten. (Anything over 1,000 is quite good.) He was slowly becoming a Grand Master. Then it happened. Jason stopped progressing in his chess ability. The players he previously had beaten in tournaments were beginning to outplay him. His game found a stalemate while his peers continued to progress. Frustrated and depressed about his game, he went to a few new instructors, but nothing seemed to work. His game had reached an endless plateau. Sadly, he left the game before he became a teenager.

One of the greatest joys in learning a new skill is advancing in your ability. Improvement breeds interest and interest in turn promotes improvement.

Unfortunately, plateaus are inevitable on the learning trail. You will see vast improvement at first. Then, more likely than not, you will plateau for a period of time. After a while, you will see a little more improvement before you will plateau again. Sometimes plateaus can last for weeks, months, or even years.

The cycle can be frustrating to any child learning a new skill. When a child is stuck in a plateau, he may lose interest or quit the activity. The fun leaves the field when you continue to play at the same level without getting any better.

Understanding why we have plateaus in the learning cycle can shed insight on how we can break free of a given plateau. The learning cycle, with its ups and downs, has many parallels to the principles of muscle building. Overall, the human body is an amazingly adaptive mechanism. When we lift weights, we force our muscles beyond normal levels, or, in other words, we stress out our muscles. (This process is called overloading the muscle.) As an adaptive response to counteract this overload, muscles produce more protein, stimulating an increase in muscle fibers.

Our muscles will stop growing unless they are continually overloaded. That is, we will have plateaus in muscle growth if the force placed upon the muscles does not change. To experience muscle growth, you can add more weight to your routine, add more repetitions, or change your exercises. When you change these workout variables, your body is designed to respond with more muscle growth.

Just as muscles respond to overload, your child can break out of a plateau if she adds new variables to the learning equation. One particular variable is stress.

Avoiding stress will not make your child a better performer, and may actually hurt her performance. Getting her out of balance and pushing her to the limit will make your child grow both mentally and emotionally. This good stress, called *eustress*, forces her body and mind to adapt, making her grow beyond her current level of performance. The following suggestions will help your child stress for success and leap over her plateaus.

↻ Seek Out Stressful Situations

Scientists at NASA routinely present their astronauts with new and catastrophic events in the flight simulator. This exercise not only prepares them for the unexpected, but it also continually advances their ability to deal with difficult situations. Gerry Griffin, crew member of *Apollo 13*, said that the mental anguish he faced in training pushed him so that he could deal effectively with the nightmare of that flight. More important, this training helped him save the lives that were at stake on that particular mission.

To rocket your child to the next level, encourage her to play against competitors who are superior to her. For instance, if she is a tennis player who wins frequently at the high school level, urge her to play open events for women. If your son is doing well in the fourteen-and-under group in golf tournaments, see if he can play a few events in the eighteen-and-under class. If your son is an accomplished golfer, recommend that he try to qualify for a professional event.

Try this same principle with music. Encourage your daughter to play a few pieces on her instrument that she believes extend her ability. These difficult musical pieces will likely be filled with many errors, many more than usual. But, in the long run, that push should make her a better musician.

This same principle of push can be applied at the academic level. Perhaps your daughter can take a few college or AP courses while still in high school. Those courses should be tougher than her usual classes, but it will make her regular high school classes seem like a breeze.

Remember, it is okay if your children fail or do poorly at these challenges. The purpose of this process is not to succeed as much as to place an overload of stress on the current level of performance, which in turn should help young people reach higher levels in the future.

↻ Change Something

Simple acts of change can promote stress. Starting a new school, moving to a new location, or taking a vacation can be stressful.

Attempting new and innovative roles also causes stress in actors. Sir Laurence Olivier, considered by many as the greatest actor of all time, started out on stage as a Shakespearean actor. According to Olivier, he played a variety of roles (from Hamlet to a crazed dentist) as a vehicle to continue his growth as an actor. He believed he would go stale and stagnant if he did not continually change his roles as well as his acting style.

To add some eustress in your daughter's life, change something that needs changing. Perhaps she should change her instructor. If she has been seeing the same instructor and her game is stagnant, it may be time for a change. Or perhaps make an equipment change. Just a new look can create a better feeling.

Make sure she plays and performs at different venues. If she always plays and practices at the same golf course, have her mix it up with more challenging courses.

If she is a tennis player, she probably practices with the same players. Have her mix up her playing partners as well. Have her practice and play against a few different opponents every once in a while.

⇨ Get Smarter

Just like our muscles grow from overload, so does our brain. Thus, if we continue to challenge our mental capacities, we should get smarter.

Make sure your daughter is continually challenging her brain. School may be challenging, but it may not be enough. Perhaps you can do a *New York Times* crossword puzzle together or create a story together. Not only will these brain-powered activities help your daughter's mental capacity, but they may give you a few more IQ points as well!

⇨ Avoid Too Much Stress

A further note on stress is needed. Our muscles need time to recover. If we lift weights every day, there is no time for our muscles to rebuild and grow: Lifting weights without a substantial break is counterproductive to our muscle growth.

Too much stress on your daughter—getting her out of balance for too long—can cause burnout. To allow her to continually grow mentally and emotionally, there must be a down time or recovery period. Make sure there are some times when she is just taking it easy, playing an easy opponent, playing an easy course, performing an easy piece on her clarinet. Encourage your daughter to alternate between periods of stress and recovery times to see the greatest gains in learning.

39

COMMIT TO EXCELLENCE

Almost 150 years ago, a man of commitment may have saved our country. His name was Joshua Chamberlain. Originally a teacher, he was made a colonel for the Twentieth Maine when he enlisted in the Union army.

While Chamberlain's division fought many battles, it was his commitment to stand firm at the Battle of Gettysburg that may have changed our country's destiny. His forces were positioned on one of the main lookout hills at Gettysburg, and his commanding general told him that whatever happened, he was not to lose the hill. The general further mentioned that keeping this hill was the key to winning this battle: If the Confederate forces captured the hill, then they could attack the Union soldiers from the rear and surround the army.

As the battle raged, with the Confederates continually charging the hill time and time again, Chamberlain's forces ran out of ammunition. His troops recommended that they retreat. Even his brother, who was a sergeant for the Twentieth Maine, suggested they retreat.

But Chamberlain refused. With all his heart he was committed to keeping this hill for the Union army. As the Confederate army approached once more to capture the hill, Chamberlain shouted, "Fix the bayonets!" Then he yelled for his men to charge.

The Rebels were in shock. They could not believe that the Union forces would charge. The Rebels thought that the Union army must have had massive reinforcements to contemplate such a bold move. In their minds it was unthinkable that a beaten regiment would charge.

While many of the Confederates turned and ran, many of them laid down their weapons and surrendered. Less than ten minutes after that charge, the Twentieth Maine had captured more than four hundred Confederate soldiers.

Some experts have said that if the Union army had lost the Battle of Gettysburg, the tide would have turned and the South would have won the war. But the South lost at Gettysburg, and, ultimately, the Civil War. The commitment of one man, Joshua Chamberlain, changed our nation's history.

Commitment breeds determination. Chamberlain was determined at all costs not to lose that hill. To reach the pinnacle in any field, commitment is a must. Whether it is athletics, science, or politics, commitment is required to attain excellence.

Vince Lombardi, the famous Green Bay Packer football coach, once said, "The quality of a person's life is in direct proportion to their commitment to excellence, regardless of their chosen field of endeavor." Mia Hamm, the famed soccer player, would agree wholeheartedly with Lombardi's statement. Mia believes not so much in her ability, but in her commitment to the cause of improving her skills.

Parents know that their children would be successful in any field if they had a level of commitment like Joshua Chamberlain or Mia Hamm. Unfortunately, that type of commitment in children is rare.

Although commitment must come from within, parents can help influence commitment with the right strategies. The following are some recommendations for helping your children develop commitment that is strong enough to "hold the hill."

↻ Discover Historic Commitment

Discuss with your child other important events, besides Joshua Chamberlain's story, that changed the direction of history. Perhaps it was an invention or a political stance. Illustrate to your child how commitment to a cause can produce historic changes.

✪ Commit to a Contract

Getting better grades is a difficult task. It can take hard work as well as commitment. Usually, spending more time studying will result in better grades. However, some children may need a light push toward spending more time at the books rather than watching television or listening to music.

Developing a contract with your child can be the needed gentle push toward an increase in study time. This contract should state items such as:

1. How much time she will spend studying each night.
2. When she will study (for example, Sunday through Thursday from 7 to 9 p.m.).
3. The benefits of studying (for example, getting into her college of choice, becoming a doctor, etc.).
4. A reward at the end of a given time period (for example, the semester) for sticking with the program. Discuss together what an appropriate reward would be. Making sure the reward is both enticing and appropriate is a vital step in the process.

Both parent and child should sign the contract. By signing the contract, the level of commitment to the program should increase.

✪ Commit to Pictures

Besides a contract, another method to enhance commitment is to use pictures and reminders of a desired outcome. If your daughter wants to be a doctor, ask her to cut out pictures of doctors from magazines. Then post these images around the house as reminders of her program and her goals. Once commitment is fortified, any battle can be won.

PART 6

EMOTIONAL BALANCE: FIND YOUR PEACE

Successful individuals diversify their talents and possess emotional balance. Their life's plate is full of wonderful activities. But people with balance like Paul McCartney and Annika Sorenstam accept their life when events do not go as planned.

A balanced life, however, is more than just winning victories—laughter, joy, and self-mastery are also must-haves. We must also give back to our communities to have a sense of balance and perspective.

Does your child have balance and perspective? Does he know how to accept the bad with the good? Can he remain calm in the vise of pressure?

This section shows how to develop balance in your child's life and how to find peace in a chaotic world.

40

LET IT BE

As Charles Dickens wrote in *The Tale of Two Cities*, "It was the best of times; it was the worst of times." Life cycles through many peaks and valleys. We all have highs and lows. It happens to all of us.

While Paul McCartney had many highs in his career, the year 1968 was a difficult time. The Beatles' career was winding down and they were getting closer and closer to breaking up. Living as a single man at that time, he was staying up too late, drinking, clubbing, and wasting his life away. As Paul puts it, he was depressed and not feeling too good about himself at this stage in his life.

One night, he had the most comforting dream about his mother, Mary, who had died when he was only fourteen. He could barely remember her face. But in this dream, her face was crystal clear, particularly her eyes. She said only three words to him in a gentle, reassuring voice: "Let it be."

He awoke with a great feeling. Paul felt that his mother had given him the message he so desperately needed: It will all work out. Just go with the flow—just let it be.

He went over to the piano and started writing his famous lyric, "When I find myself in times of trouble, Mother Mary comes to me, speaking words of wisdom, let it be, let it be."

This song became his anthem, one of the songs for which he is most well known. As Paul described it, "Writing this song felt like magic."

The philosophy of "let it be" can help us accept the ups and downs that we all experience in a competition, a season, and even a career. Life is great when we are on top. This is when we have supreme confidence in ourselves and everything goes our way.

But we all will go through a lull. Unfortunately, once the downward slide begins, many people lose their resolve and may even panic. Others begin to doubt themselves, losing their belief in their abilities. With that type of mind-set, their downward slide will persist longer, possibly turning into a nasty slump.

We have to accept the times when we are struggling and just go with the flow—just let it be. The following mental tool will help your child accomplish this "go with the flow" mentality.

⟳ Be Like Mike

Adopting the mind-set of Michael Jordan, one of the all-time great basketball players, can help a child be more accepting of highs and lows in performance.

Michael Jordan went with the flow because he was a great basketball statistician. At certain times during a game, Michael knew that he would miss some shots, perhaps several in a row. However, he kept on shooting because he knew that he would eventually get on a hot streak again.

Statisticians know about percentages and Michael knew that basketball percentages are tallied by misses and makes. Further, Michael seemingly knew that misses and makes come in clusters.

Just as mathematicians will tell you, statistics is simple. Let's say Michael averaged 70 percent from the field. That does not mean he would hit 7 shots in a row and then miss 3. Rather he would have many different sequences of hits and misses. One sequence could be 2 misses followed by 6 hits, followed by 3 misses, then 7 hits, then 1 miss. The sequence can have many different variations. But at the end of the season when you add up the hits and misses, you will get 7 hits for every 10 shots attempted.

To have your child be more like Mike, first figure out your child's percentage in some performance. It could be a batting average, field goal percentage, or number of As and Bs they get on tests.

Next, create a pattern of hits and misses reflective of this percentage. For instance, let's say your child has a batting average of .250. Have your child write out a series of hits and misses, with X equaling hits and 0 equaling misses. As an example, create a string of 40 attempts that equates to the .250 batting average, with 10 hits for every 40 at bats. In this case, the sequence may look like this:

XXOOOOOOOXXOOOOOOOOOOXXXXOOOOOOOOOOXOOOX

Last, discuss with your child the many patterns that can occur. For instance, there is a time during this sequence that your child did not get a hit in 10 attempts. Let him understand that this mini-slump is normal: It is just the way it can play out. By plotting out such a sequence, it will be apparent that highs and lows are the way the ball typically bounces in a season.

The same statistical principle can be applied to a B student in Spanish. This student may get a few Cs on tests and perhaps even one D, but perhaps several As.

Teach your child not to second-guess himself or lose composure during the worst of times. Emphasize that the best of times are right around the corner. As Paul McCartney would tell us, it is important to just let it be.

41

FIND THE JOY

Willie Stargell, a former baseball player for the Pittsburgh Pirates, pointed out that umpires started the game by shouting "Play ball!"—not by yelling "Work ball!" Willie loved to play baseball, but more importantly, he realized that his level of play would be much higher if he enjoyed what he was doing. Dusty Baker, a great player for the Dodgers in the 1970s, held similar beliefs. Dusty would recall all the great times he had as a kid playing ball in his backyard and would bring those pleasant thoughts to the plate with him.

When Bill Bradley speaks about basketball, it is as if he speaks about a dear friend. "I felt about the court, the ball, the basket, the way people feel about friends," he wrote in his book *The Values of the Game*. Bradley commented that he played his best when he allowed the kid inside to come out and feel the joy of the game. He further mentioned that he played for the pure exhilaration of shooting and passing. To Bradley, the score was always secondary to the joy of the game. The importance of finding the joy in your sport is nothing new. The ancient Chinese philosopher Chuan Tzu knew this to be true and wrote many years ago:

> *When archers shoot for enjoyment, they have all their skill,*
> *When they shoot for a brass buckle, they get nervous,*
> *When they shoot for a prize of gold, they begin to see two targets.*

If you want your child to perform her best under pressure, finding joy in the activity is essential. As Tzu believed, enjoying the task is one of the greatest antidotes against pressure and stress.

Fun and stress do not mix; they are like oil and water. Pleasure in the action, however, will help remove the pressure from the day.

Parents should encourage their children to believe that the pleasure of the performance must be greater than the pressure of the performance. The pro golfer Davis Love III once mentioned the most important advice he ever received from his father: "Follow your dream and enjoy the trip."

The following drills will help parents promote the pleasure of the journey in their child.

⟳ Make a Joy List

Your child gravitated toward his hobby or sport for many reasons, and one of those must have been enjoyment. Sometimes the pressure makes us lose sight of the pleasure. To emphasize the pleasure, ask your son to make a list of ten reasons why he likes certain activities such as playing his musical instrument or playing his sport. You may want to have him make up a joy list for all his activities.

Next, figure out ways to enhance the joy in your child's life. For instance, if your son said that he enjoys seeing himself improve his skills on the piano, make sure the feedback you give him reflects skill mastery. Focus on activities that can further his improvement. Also, create goals with him that emphasize skill improvement.

If the list includes his joy of social outlets on his soccer team, then emphasize his friendships. Perhaps ensure that he has enough time before and after the game to socialize with his friends on the team.

POSSESS INTEGRITY
ABOVE ALL ELSE

While walking with friends to the concession stands at the Friday night football game, Jake spotted a wallet. He picked it up and opened the billfold to find three crisp hundred-dollar bills. His friends happily announced he had found the jackpot and they were going to have a great time after the game.

But Jake said that he was going to return it to the concession stand. His friends could not believe their ears and tried to deter him. But Jake replied, "My dad lost his wallet last week, and I saw the look of joy and relief on his face when someone returned it to him, with all the money. Sorry, but I need to return this wallet."

Just as he approached the concession stand, a man rushed up to the cashier with a desperate look on his face, asking about a lost wallet. Jake, with a big smile, turned to the man and gave him the wallet. The man then opened the wallet and saw the $300 as well as all his credit cards. He then handed Jake one of the hundred-dollar bills and said how impressed he was with Jake's honesty and integrity.

Jake discovered that night how one good deed deserves another.

Most parents want their children to act with the utmost integrity. Most parents would cherish the moment their children acted like Jake; they would believe they had done their job well if their children valued their integrity more than money and valued integrity more than winning an important event or gaining an advantage over the competition.

Joe Paterno, the Penn State football coach, once said, "Success without honor is an unseasoned dish: It will satisfy your hunger, but it won't taste good." Instilling integrity and honor in children is vital if we want them to feel good about their actions. Unfortunately, our children see many mixed messages in the media about winning at all costs. Our children have plenty of role models who cross the integrity line.

Take the 2006 World Series as an example. Many of the players for the St. Louis Cardinals questioned whether Kenny Rogers, a pitcher on the Detroit Tigers, was using pine tar to gain an advantage. The allegation was never proven, only suggested; Rogers denied the allegation and said he had only used dirt and rosin to muddy up the ball. The umpires did not pursue the matter.

But cheating has long been associated with baseball. At the turn of the century the White Sox threw the 1919 series for a few extra bucks, forever to be known as the Black Sox Scandal. Recently, steroids in baseball has been a problem. Barry Bonds has never admitted to knowingly taking them. Rather, he blames his trainer for his transgression. And the home run king, Mark McGwire, brushes off comments about his possible steroid use.

Cheating in baseball is only the tip of the moral iceberg in sports. We can point our finger at other professional sports as well. On any given Sunday, there will be holding on every play on the NFL line of scrimmage. Holding will significantly slow down the pass rush, so many offensive players will try to get away with this transgression in order to win. But cheating also happens on the hardwood. Some players will travel with the basketball as much as possible, knowing the refs will let it ride most of the time.

Examples of moral ineptitude are not just reserved for sports. Look at Enron, where corporate leaders bilked millions of dollars from their employees. Jeff Skilling, the CEO at Enron, expressed remorse when he was found guilty, but still believes he did nothing wrong.

We are in a battle for our children's integrity. In a recent survey on ethics in children, 60 percent of American high school students said they have cheated on a test. In addition, 62 percent said they lied to a teacher in the past twelve months and 81 percent said they lied to a parent. Ethics is definitely a problem with young people.

Unfortunately, there are many poor role models for our children to emulate. If our children see professional athletes cheating and leaders of corporations stealing, the chances are greater our children will do the same.

Fortunately, parents play the most important role in encouraging integrity, both on and off the field. While children have heroes on television, the real influence starts outside of that box, at home with the parents. The following drills show parents how to place a premium on integrity in their children.

⇨ Let Integrity Flow from All Directions

Arthur Gordon, a politician and author, once said, "In mathematics, an integer is a number that isn't divided into fractions. Just so, a man of integrity isn't divided against himself." A person does not have integrity once in a while or just in some situations. A person of integrity has integrity all the time and in all situations.

To explain this principle to your children, get a straw and cut it into three parts. Tell them that the first part relates to having integrity in school—which means not cheating on tests or having someone else do your homework. The second part relates to relationships—telling the truth rather than lying to your friends or parents to get what you want. The third part relates to sports or an activity like music—being a good sport about winning and losing as well as not cheating to win.

Now tape the straw back together and see if it works. Of course it will not: Air will escape and make the straw useless. Explain to your children that the straw is like our integrity. We cannot have integrity in just one area in our life. For us to have integrity flow in our lives, we need to plug up all the holes by exhibiting integrity in all situations.

⇨ Discuss What-If Scenarios

Discuss different situations that will test your child's integrity. Play "what-if" and discuss how he might respond. Also, discuss the consequences of his actions. Here is a list of what-if scenarios related to integrity:

- What if you were given answers to the test?
- What if your friend asked you to help him cheat?

- What if you find a wallet with $300 in it?
- What if you see a homeless person lying on the ground?
- What if you need the point to win the match and your opponent's shot hits inside the tennis line, but the umpire called it out?

These are just a few examples. Make up a list relevant to your child. It will create some meaningful discussions.

DIVERSIFY YOUR INTERESTS

Hurry up! Hurry up! We are going to be late for soccer practice, and then I have to drop your sister off at cheerleading," Jack's mother said, "and then I have to take you to piano lessons and your sister to violin lessons."

Such an interaction plays out in most homes across America on many days. Typically, parents want to expose their children to as many wonderful experiences as possible, believing that participation in lots of activities creates balance and perspective. Most importantly, parents think that balance and perspective are key ingredients to living a full and happy life.

A balanced life gives Venus Williams, the former number one women's tennis player, a sense of comfort. During a television interview at the 2003 U.S. Open, the commentator asked Venus how she felt about her injury withdrawal from the tournament. Venus had lost in the 2002 finals, and the commentator wondered if she was anxious to get back into competition. With a glow reserved for enlightened individuals, Venus mentioned that she felt disappointed yet eternally happy. She then spoke with joy about her new interior design company and her new tennis clothing line. Venus Williams is much more than just one of the greatest tennis players of all time. Venus has a full plate of life.

But having too many activities and "too full a plate of life" can become problematic for children. A line exists between encouraging your children to participate in a few activities and shoving them into an onslaught of activities. Parents who want their children to have a balanced life need to be careful not to push their children into a stressed out, out-of-balance, chaotic life, with too many activities.

Given this important issue, a key question is, "How many activities are appropriate for my children?"

Sport psychologists have been studying young athletes for more than twenty years. These investigations have discovered vital information related to raising a successful and happy child. Unfortunately, most of the information lies in academic journals unread by the eyes of its most important audience—parents.

One such study that has marvelous application to parenting involves tennis players from Sweden in the 1980s. Twenty years ago, men's tennis was dominated by the likes of Bjorn Borg, Stefan Edberg, and Mats Wilander. Sport scientists wanted to discover how such a small country inhabited by a few people could dominate an international sport. To decipher this mystery, researchers investigated the differences between the tennis players who achieved international greatness and those who never moved beyond the amateur ranks.

This investigation yielded one essential finding related to the number of activities that are appropriate for developing excellence. The successful tennis players in the study participated in three different sports, such as soccer, ice hockey, and tennis. However—and this point is key—when these athletes turned fifteen, they played only tennis. Interestingly, the unsuccessful athletes competed in only tennis throughout their younger formative years.

Participating in a variety of activities can promote excellence in two significant ways. First, playing a variety of sports can help with motor development. The young athlete learns to develop coordination skills that can transfer to other sports. For instance, playing soccer at a young age can contribute to better footwork on the tennis court. Second, diversification also can reduce pressure. If a child participates in only one activity, there is a need to always perform well in that activity and get those "self-esteem points." However, if a child plays a variety of sports, or participates in a variety of activities, then there is less pressure to always perform well. He can feel good about himself from a number of activities and hobbies, and thus the pressure is off to perform well in every situation.

This diversification principle will hold true for your child. The following are a few recommendations to help diversify your child's talents.

○ Create Ambidexterity

When Michelangelo was working on the Sistine Chapel, he would switch his hands to paint that famous ceiling. Although Michelangelo actually was ambidextrous, he believed in the importance of developing balance in his abilities.

Suggest to your son that he become balanced across his extremities. If he plays golf right-handed, have him hit a few balls from the left side every time he practices. The same philosophy would apply to other sports, such as baseball or soccer. Players should practice swinging and kicking from both sides.

○ Decrease Injuries

Participating in a variety of sports and activities can reduce the chance of injuries. When your child uses the same muscles and tendons for the same activity, overuse and injuries can occur. Participation in a variety of activities gives your child time to heal and rest certain muscles and tendons, decreasing the chance of injury.

○ Create Appropriate Balance

Given the study described in this chapter, it seems appropriate that parents should have their children focus on three different activities. This may be soccer, playing the piano, and acting in the school play. Focusing on more than that number may be unnecessary and possibly counterproductive.

Ask your child which three activities she likes. Focus on those with great energy and passion. Eventually, your child will gravitate toward the activity in which she is most talented and enjoys the best.

Parents certainly should not feel guilty about having their children participate in just a few activities every year! They should be relieved to know that a relatively small list of activities trumps an endless round of hobbies.

Balance Competition and Mastery

It seems like the mantra for our country is "Winning is not everything, winning is the only thing." Many Americans care only about winning: Second place or just competing is not good enough. Do we celebrate who lost in the playoffs in baseball, basketball, or football? Do we even remember which team lost the Super Bowl two years ago?

Olympic athletes who win the gold are typically bestowed with wealth, respect, and fame. The athletes who win a silver or bronze medal are usually forgotten very quickly. Our children get the message that being number one is the only goal that matters.

Not all cultures value being number one, however. Some Eastern cultures value self-mastery as the main key to enlightenment. There's a story that illustrates this philosophy. An American tourist found himself in Asia on the day of a pilgrimage to the top of a sacred mountain. Thousands of village people would climb to the mountaintop. The tourist, who had been active all his life and was in great shape, decided to join the pilgrimage. After twenty minutes, he was out of breath and could hardly climb another step, yet the elderly and the young villagers moved easily past him. "I don't understand it," he said to his Asian companion. "How can all these villagers easily climb the mountain, while it is so difficult for me?"

His friend answered, "You have the typical American attitude and you see everything as a competition. You see the mountain as your enemy and you set out to conquer it. So naturally the mountain fights back. The mountain will always be stronger than you. However, our culture does not see the mountain as our enemy but as a friend—a friend that will guide us along the way. The purpose of our climb is to enjoy the mountain and learn from it, and so it lifts us up and carries us along."

When the goal is to be the best and winning is the only concern, then this pressure can feel like a mountain weighing you down. Most people are not the best, and in most cases, only half the people on the field can win. Consequently, the quest for victory can become insurmountable for those who rarely win.

Researchers have found that children who focus on being better than their peers can have less confidence and enjoyment in the activity, especially when they are not winning. Focusing primarily upon competitive goals also can contribute to dropping out of the activity.

Alternatively, studies have shown that when a person focuses on self-improvement rather than being the best and winning, a substantial increase in confidence and motivation occurs as well as a boost in performance. A focus on mastery can even improve sportsmanship behavior. Alternatively, when parents emphasize winning as the highest priority, children internalize that value and may do what it takes to be a winner. In many cases, that leads to cheating and lying. Further, when parents emphasize winning as the premium value, children feel bad when they do not win, causing them to handle losing in a less-than-gracious way.

However, we must not entirely discourage focusing on being the best. In some cases, a focus on winning is essential. Many great performers value being the best and thrive on that need. Trying to be the best in your class, the best on your team, or the best in the orchestra can stoke the fire that drives those long hours of practice. Without it, many would lose their desire to compete.

To help a child perform at the highest levels, there should be a balance between mastery and competitive outlooks. Both objectives can feed off one another, helping your child reach even higher levels of success than focusing upon one or the other. Some researchers have found that a combination of objectives creates the best path to excellence.

Such a strategy worked for Nick Faldo. In the mid-1980s Nick was one of the best golfers in Europe. However, he wanted to be known as one of the best golfers in the world. To accomplish this, a golfer must win major tournaments. Unfortunately, Nick's swing did not hold up under the pressure of major championship golf. As fortune would have it, Nick connected with David Leadbetter, who rebuilt Nick's swing piece by piece.

But this was not an easy path for Nick. For the next few years his game fell off the charts and so did his ranking. During this period, Nick was willing to downplay his competitive objectives and focused mainly on mastering his new swing.

Ultimately all the hard work on his new swing paid off. In 1989 he won his first Masters, a golfing major, and has since captured five more majors as well as been elected to the golf Hall of Fame. By emphasizing both learning and competitive objectives, Nick became an all-time great.

Most parents want their children to be successful. Some parents focus solely on having their children become the best, while others want their children to have fun and master the skill.

Perhaps the issue should not be whether a mastery or competitive objective is more conducive to performance. But rather, when these objectives should be implemented. That is, it may be a timing issue. Sometimes a mastery focus is appropriate and sometimes competitive objectives would help achievement.

Parents need to judge which objective is warranted based on the child as well as the situation. Balance your feedback in both regards and you will end up with a well-balanced child, full of fun and the desire to win. The following drills focus on creating a balance between both mastery and competitive objectives.

⇨ Learn to Value Competition

What happens when a child focuses only upon having fun when the environment is highly competitive?

The child will likely feel out of place.

A focus on mastery is appropriate at certain times, but during competition fun is not enough. If your child focuses primarily on fun and mastery, praise those objectives, but also emphasize the possibility of winning. Discuss with your child the benefits of a competitive outlook.

Possible questions to discuss with your child include:

- Does winning fuel your desire to practice?

- Do you enjoy being the best in your class?
- Does winning feel good to you? Why?
- Why is being one of the best trumpet players in the band important?

Also, you should sprinkle in some competitive goals for a mastery-oriented child. For instance, you could set a goal with your son to be in the top 50 percent of his class, or win at least half his soccer games, or be in the top half of the best violinists in his orchestra. Once these goals are reached, set more challenging competitive goals. This creates a balance between mastery and competitive objectives.

⟳ Master Your World

What happens when a child emphasizes winning at all costs and is not the best? What happens when being number one is key, but your child is only a benchwarmer?

This can be highly problematic. It can lead to distress and possible burnout, especially when your child is not victorious. In this case, parents should emphasize the importance of mastery. If your child did not win the match or perform at his best, then discuss what can be learned from the event. A parent can always find some mastery objectives to focus upon within the competitive environment. Possible questions to discuss with your child include:

- Did your second serve percentage improve?
- Did you answer the essay questions better this time?
- Did you recite your lines in the audition with more passion, even though you did not get the part in the play?

With a highly competitive child, the parent should include a few mastery goals during the semester. These could include improving her free throw percentage by 10 percent, reading one more book than her typical average each semester, and hitting 20 percent more fairways during her golf tournaments.

45

FUND YOUR SELF-ESTEEM

After getting an education in economics in the United States, Muhammed Yunus went back to his home country of Bangladesh to make a difference. Armed with knowledge, he believed he could make a significant change in his country through microcredit. He founded Grameen Bank and began to give small loans to poor people, up to $300.

Muhammed understood that even small sums could help people to begin a business. Loans as low as $9 have helped beggars start small businesses and poor women buy basket-weaving materials.

But the loan recipients gained much more than material wealth with this process. Muhammed realized that this loan gave the recipients a new sense of empowerment. It showed that someone believed in them, which gave them dignity and helped them feel good about themselves. The loan was not just about buying materials: It provided a boost to their self-esteem as well.

For his work, Muhammed was awarded the Nobel Peace Prize in 2006. The committee said, "Lasting peace cannot be achieved unless large groups find ways in which to break out of poverty. Development from below also serves to advance democracy and human rights."

A rise in self-esteem can change the direction of a nation. A boost in self-esteem in a child can change his destiny. Parents continually struggle to raise their children's self-esteem. Typically, parents want their children to feel a sense of empowerment and to believe that their actions will make a difference. Most parents know that high self-esteem is the key to success.

In the past, experts encouraged rewards and positive feedback to boost self-esteem. When used appropriately, praise can boost self-esteem.

Specifically, praise and rewards should be given if a child acts in a competent way, such as making a good play in baseball or receiving a good grade on a test.

Unfortunately, praise can diminish a child's self-esteem if used haphazardly. When praise is given for an ordinary action that is not necessarily worthy of praise, it can decrease a child's confidence. Praise can be counterproductive if given to a child all the time.

The current belief is that to boost self-esteem, we must focus upon challenging young minds. More importantly, self-esteem will be bolstered when children know how they can meet these challenges. Constructive criticism shows children how to effectively meet these challenges.

Theodore Leschetizky, the great piano teacher, once said, "We learn much from disagreeable things people say, for they make us think, whereas the good things only make us glad." Leschetizky knew that building self-esteem takes much more than just praise. We can feel better about ourselves when we get a taste of criticism, because criticism makes us evaluate our actions. We improve from criticism, while praise often encourages us to repeat our actions not help us to progress.

While constructive criticism is essential to building self-esteem, if it is given excessively, your child will tune you out. To decrease this possibility, a parent should use praise to open the door of engagement. That is, praise and criticism should be given together as a vehicle for change. The following drill illustrates how to balance praise with constructive feedback.

⟳ Nourish Self-esteem with the Sandwich Approach

With the sandwich approach, praise is first given in regards to a specific behavior that the child performs well. Then criticism is given related to what the parent would like to change. The message ends with a form of praise about some related competency.

Here are some examples of the sandwich approach:

- *I like how you have arranged your shirts on the closet shelf. I believe you can get your sock drawer a little neater, however. Your room looks*

100 percent better. I appreciate the effort you made to tidy your room before your cousins come to visit.

- *I like the way you bent your knees to make that catch. Be a little lighter on your feet the next time the ball is hit to you. You are really getting good at this position.*
- *You had nice rhythm at your recital. I think you need to extend some notes a little longer. You are very close to playing that piece just like the composer wrote it.*
- *You are treating your brother nicer today. Still try to limit the put-downs. Keep up the brotherly attitude!*

Building self-esteem closely parallels the old proverb about self-sufficiency and fishing: If you give a hungry person a fish, he will eat for a day. If you teach a hungry person how to fish, he will eat for a lifetime.

To continue the fishing analogy: To effectively build self-esteem in your child, praise him when he puts the lure in the water. But also correct his mistakes so that he becomes proficient at fishing. When he reaches a certain level of proficiency, take him to more challenging fishing holes. Then, in due time, he will believe he is a great fisherman.

46

Go Slow

For months, Vanessa had practiced her favorite Beethoven piece for this audition. But today, when it really mattered, at her audition for Juilliard, Vanessa did not have the magic. Her timing and rhythm were off, and she played the piece much faster than Beethoven had intended.

After the audition, Vanessa's piano instructor asked her what happened. Vanessa responded, "Everything seemed to go too fast. My fingers moved too fast, my eyes moved too fast, and my brain moved at light speed. All of this made my timing go out of whack and it just made me goof up."

Vanessa had succumbed to the powers of anxiety. When we are anxious, we release hormones such as epinephrine and norepinephrine, which act as stimulants. When we are anxious, we typically do everything faster. We walk and talk faster. These hormones can make our fingers move faster as well as speed up our thinking, as it did for Vanessa. These hormones, then, are the cause of Vanessa's poor playing.

Hormones released by our anxious thoughts will not only affect the play on a piano. They can disrupt a good golf swing or a great pitching motion as well as ruin our test-taking abilities. All in all, these hormones need to be controlled with appropriate thoughts and behaviors. The following mental tools will help children combat the increased speed resulting from these hormones.

➲ Slow Down Under Pressure

Gary Player, one of the all-time great golfers, knows about this high speed problem during competition. To combat this potential problem, he developed a unique mental strategy: He does everything at a slower pace before a tournament. He meanders to the practice tee and even ties his shoes unhurriedly before a tournament round.

Gary's strategy is quite ingenious. While his movements may feel slower to him, Gary actually moves at normal speeds. This strategy counterbalances the speed increase caused by his hormones, and he breaks even on his quickness.

Have your children slow down in pressure-packed endeavors. If your daughter has an audition like Vanessa's, have her slow down. Suggest that she get her instrument out of the case a little bit slower. Have her put her music sheets on the stand a little slower and to overall move a little more slowly before she begins her play.

If your son plays golf, apply the philosophy that Gary Player does under the gun of competition. Suggest that he walk gingerly over to the practice tee. Suggest that he take some slow practice swings and warm up at a very deliberate pace. Once he is ready, tell him to approach the tee as if his feet were in molasses. When he is ready to hit his first tee shot, tell him to think about doing everything a little slower, from his practice swings to the execution of the opening tee shot.

Being slow under pressure should speed up your child's success.

47

WHISTLE YOUR WAY
TO THE TOP

"Just breathe," Craig thought. "Just breathe." He could see that his daughter Hilary's face was almost purple as she tried to answer the questions in a Junior Jeopardy contest at her school. When the emcee asked her a question, Hilary would hold her breath and grimace as she thought about the answer. Usually gifted in the trivia department, Hilary faltered, rarely answering any of the questions. Craig knew his daughter had choked, both literally and figuratively, from how she was breathing during the contest.

Hilary reacted like most people do under pressure—we have a tendency not to breathe appropriately. This reaction is natural in a fearful situation. When we experience anxiety, our breathing becomes more shallow and hasty. In some instances, it may even stop entirely.

The consequence of shallow or subdued breathing is a reduction of oxygen to our brain. In turn, we may lose our concentration and decrease our mental acuity, as in Hilary's case. This inappropriate breathing will also make our muscles tighten up and we may lose our ability to control our body. Further, shallow breathing due to anxiety can restrict the blood flow to the extremities. When this occurs, we can lose our sense of touch and feel, which can greatly limit our skill in sports or in music.

While your children know how to breathe, they may not do it effectively. The following drills will help parents teach their children to use more oxygen under pressure and avoid the choking response, literally and figuratively.

○ Take Deep Breaths Under Pressure

Your daughter may hold her breath under pressure or take shallow breaths. Neither will work under pressure. The key is to learn how to take a few deep breaths when the pressure hits.

To illustrate how to breathe effectively, first ask her to place her index finger on her belly button. Then have her move her finger three inches toward her head while still touching her stomach. Next she should lift her finger up from her stomach, about a half inch off the skin. As she inhales, her stomach should hit her finger. Explain to her that a deep breath feels this big. Also, suggest to her that while she is breathing, she should visualize all this good air entering her body and filling up her lungs. Under pressure, she wants to make sure she is taking in enough oxygen and breathing deeply.

○ Whistle While You Play

Under pressure, sometimes we just forget to breathe. Whistling is a good strategy to combat this problem. Fuzzy Zoeller, the PGA pro, does this throughout a round. You can hear Fuzzy belting out a tune down the fairway.

Whistling forces us to breathe deeply. When we whistle, air is being forced out to make sound, using the diaphragm—which is key to breathing deeply. Experts recommend that people with respiratory difficulties breathe as if they are whistling.

Suggest to your son that he try whistling a light tune when under pressure. Perhaps he could whistle a very short tune while he is on the free throw line. In fact, a short whistle could be part of his routine. Or invite him to try humming a tune, which also will promote deep breathing.

Whether your child has music in him or not, just make sure he keeps breathing under pressure.

FIND SERENITY NOW

Give me the strength to accept the things I cannot control
The courage to change the things I can control
And the wisdom to know the difference between the two.
　　　　　　　　　　　　　　　　—The Serenity Prayer

Kim saw her daughter, Sammy, yelling at two cheerleaders after their dance routine during halftime. Kim could tell that Sammy was distraught and upset. On the way home, Kim asked her daughter why she was so upset.

Sammy answered, "We practice and practice and those two girls always make the same mistakes. Mom, it's really frustrating when I'm the captain. They make me look bad!"

"Sammy, we can only control our own behavior," her mother said. "We can't control other people. Just prepare the team the best you can, and then let the chips fall where they will. When you do that, you won't get so upset."

Kim was exposing a simple truth to her daughter—we should only focus on the things over which we have control and forget about the things over which we have no control. When we do that, we have a greater sense of peace.

That simple principle helps great athletes find peace inside chaos. It did for Annika Sorenstam's chaotic week in 2003 when she competed against the men on the PGA tour.

For weeks building up to the event, she made numerous appearances on a variety of television shows, from *The Late Show with David Letterman* to *The Today Show*. Everyone wanted to know why she was competing and whether she would play on the men's tour as a permanent fixture.

During the week of the event in Fort Worth, the eyes of the world fell upon her. Media came from every part of the world to cover this story. Her press conferences took hours to complete. Reporters bombarded her with questions on topics ranging from her thoughts about the course to whether she believed she could make the cut. The world wanted to know the mind of Annika.

The pressure was immense, to say the least. Annika mentioned that the pressure was analogous to competing in all four major tournaments, but in this case, they all were rolled into one.

Annika has a mental game that is one of the best in all sports. One of her mental strategies for handling pressure, and one she used at Fort Worth, involves focusing on the controllables of the game. She focuses on what she can control and disregards what she cannot. Annika has said that once the ball leaves her clubface, she ceases to worry about it. She cannot control whether the ball will take a bad bounce or good one, so she removes that concern from her mind.

Annika intuitively knows that focusing only upon the things she can control in her life reduces her stress. Psychologists have found that there is a significant relationship between feelings of control and stress level. Individuals who perceive a situation to be outside their control have higher levels of anxiety than those who believe they possess some level of control over the event.

Whether she knew it or not, Annika used a form of the Serenity Prayer to reduce the pressure during the 2003 PGA tour. As this prayer dictates, when you can accept any outcome and let go of factors outside your control such as getting bad breaks, you will find serenity under pressure. Although her play was outstanding, she missed the cut by a few strokes. Nonetheless, she gained the respect of the golfing world.

Sammy, like many children, would benefit from adopting Annika's lead and developing a mental philosophy that follows the Serenity Prayer. The following exercises illustrate to parents how they can help their children reduce their stress and anxiety by observing the principles of this prayer.

⟡ Find Your Serenity

Finding serenity in a performance setting involves a three-step process. First have your child make a list of all her worries. These can include the ability to pass an upcoming test, to play well in the band, or to score a goal in soccer.

Next have your child write the worries in two separate lists: one list for items she can control and another for items she cannot control. Discuss with your child what worries fit into the "cannot control" list. For instance, having a particular person like you is out of your control. No matter what you do, some people may not like you. Winning is out of your child's control as well. The opponent may be superior or feeling better that day and, no matter how your daughter plays, she may not win.

For the worries your child placed into the "cannot control" list, have her think like Annika. Encourage her to find the mental strength to accept those factors over which she has limited or no control. These factors must be accepted and simply let go.

If your child finds that she continually thinks about these "uncontrollables," she may benefit from using the mental tool described in the Rid Your Mind of Negative Trash drill on page 71. Have her crumple the paper with the list of uncontrollable worries and throw it in a trash can. When she starts to think about the worries, have her say, "Stop, it is in the trash can." Suggest that she do this every time she begins to think these unproductive thoughts. Eventually, she will be able to throw away all her "uncontrollable" worries.

Now, here comes the courage part. Have your daughter devise one strategy to combat each of those worries she placed on the "can control" list. For instance, if she worries about her grades being good enough for college, a strategy would be to study more or get a tutor. If she worries about her appearance, a fitness program or joining a sports team may help. Following a specified strategy for each worry not only will help your daughter achieve desired goals, it will also give her a greater sense of control over the situation, ultimately reducing her anxiety.

When your daughter learns to let go of factors she cannot control and focus only upon aspects within her control, she will discover serenity in her life.

49

LAUGH YOURSELF
TO EXCELLENCE

In most high schools, students who run for class president must make a speech at a general assembly in front of the student body. Leslie was one of those candidates. She bought a brand new pair of jeans and high heeled boots for that special occasion. When her name was called to greet the students and deliver her speech, she strode onto the stage confidently, eager for her chance to be heard. Unfortunately, Leslie did not know how slippery the stage floor was: She slipped and landed on her bottom. In shock for a few seconds, as was the audience, she then began to laugh—which told the audience that they, too, could laugh at her misfortune.

The principal asked if she was okay, and helped Leslie to her feet. Leslie gingerly walked to the podium and ad-libbed, "As you noticed from previous events, I get to the bottom of things"—and she pointed to her bottom—"and I will get to the bottom of any problems here at John F. Kennedy High." She completed her speech to resounding applause.

An ancient Chinese proverb says, "Time spent laughing is time spent with the gods." Intuitively, Leslie knows the power of laughter. By making fun of herself and bringing humor to the moment, Leslie won over the crowd. The students might not remember that speech in years to come, but they likely will remember the tumble and how graciously Leslie handled herself.

Bringing levity to a tense moment also can lighten the pressure load. The great Dallas Cowboys' quarterback Roger Staubach knew this principle and applied this to his winning style. In a pressure-packed moment in the fourth quarter of an NFC championship game, Roger went to the sideline during a timeout to get the next play from his coach, the legendary

Tom Landry. As Roger asked for the play, he saw Coach Landry looking up through the opening in the ceiling of Texas Stadium. (The stadium's roof is not completely closed, and people call the opening "God's peephole.") After a few moments, Coach Landry looked back down and called the play. At that moment, Roger replied, "Coach, I always wondered where you got those plays," and then jogged back to the huddle, chuckling all the way. Roger decreased the gravity of the moment with a little humor.

Laughter, known as the universal elixir, can be one of your child's best antidotes to a bad day. Researchers have found that laughter releases hormones such as endorphins that are considered the brain's natural opiates, giving you a sense of euphoria. In essence, laughing can make your child feel good about a bad day.

A good chuckle produces a relaxation response as well. When we laugh, our body does internal jogging: Our blood pressure surges, our heart rate increases, and we have greater muscle tension. After the laugh as well as after a jog, the body returns to normal physiological levels in a few moments. This rebound effect causes a relaxation response in our bodies.

Laughter also can increase your child's productivity. First, laughter can place us in a good mood, and we tend to have more energy when our mood is lighthearted. Second, after a good laugh, your child's mental capacities will likely increase, such as concentration levels and ability to solve difficult problems, essentials for getting good grades at school.

The power of laughter can go far beyond just enhancing the performance levels in your children. Laughter is a great medicine for their health. In *Anatomy of an Illness as Perceived by the Patient*, Norman Cousins described how he recovered from a debilitating illness by laughing himself to greater health. Norman developed a library of classic comedies and watched those movies every day. His illness disappeared, astonishing his doctors. His book and life story helped to create new support for the use of laughter as a therapy.

The choice is simple. When bad breaks happen to our children, they can choose the easy path of anger and throw a fit. They can get depressed and upset at every wrong turn and piece of bad luck. As a result, they will probably ruin their day with stress as well as destroy their health.

Given all the great benefits of laughter, parents should readily promote this response. Here are a few suggestions to increase laughter in your household.

➪ Find the Laughter

Did you know children laugh an average of four hundred times a day? But by the time they reach adulthood, this drops to twenty-five laughs a day. Does your child laugh a lot, or did he lose all the laughter with the seriousness of life?

To find more laughter, have your son count how many times he laughs a day (giggling counts). Have him conduct this calculation every day for the next week, then compare his number to the norm. If it is low, don't worry. His laughing should increase because he is now aware of it.

➪ Develop Your Own Humor Library

Develop an audiotape or videotape library of great comedy like Norman Cousins did. Make it a family goal to watch at least one comedy every week. When taking a drive with the kids, put in a comedy tape instead of listening to music. A family that laughs together, stays together.

➪ Stretch Your Mind with Laughter Yoga

You may not exercise with your children, but you can participate with them in a different kind of workout called Laughter Yoga. In this exercise, people get together and make themselves laugh for five minutes. At some point, people usually start howling with joy. The results will delight you! And this exercise will not just benefit your children—Laughter Yoga is a great release for parents as well.

When parents promote a "laughing" outlook, their children will find greater enjoyment in their life and may even live longer as a result.

Finish Strong

In 1964, Billy Mills ran one of the most incredible finishes in Olympic history. For most of the 10,000 meter race, Billy was in third. As he entered the last lap, he told himself that third place and a bronze medal would suffice. However, something clicked inside him: His champion voice began to be heard.

For years before the race, he had trained his champion voice. A Native American who was orphaned at age 12 and grew up on a reservation, Billy won an athletic scholarship to the University of Kansas, winning several titles and helping his team to two national championships. After graduation he joined the marines and gave up running for a while.

But he never lost his desire to be a champion. He wrote positive self-statements in his journal for years leading up to this big event. Some of these statements focused on feeling great on the day of the race while other statements related to having a fantastic finish. With great determination and commitment to his cause, he had mentally prepared himself for years for this one race.

As he entered the last turn, he decided third place would not be good enough and began to think, "I can win, I can win, I can win." With those words came an incredible burst of energy. Billy passed his two competitors in the final 20 meters, finishing on top of the podium, holding the gold medal.

While Billy's journey had many twists and turns along the way, he had the know-how and determination to finish strong. His journey led him to the top of his game.

This book can be the start of a wonderful journey for you and your children. It is a journey of dreams. Once the path is clear, the steps are easy.

It is a journey of change. Change is difficult and takes courage. But almost all accomplishments in life take a bit of courage.

It is a journey of excellence. Excellence takes effort, determination, and sacrifice. Think of this book as a guide. Read it again and again; once may not be enough. There are many skills in this book that take time and patience to master. But once acquired, these skills will help empower your children to achieve their potential.

I leave you with these simple words to share with your children on their way to excellence:

Find your passion.
Create the path.
Make the commitment.
Enjoy the journey.

REFERENCES

Introduction
Woods, Earl, and Fred Mitchell. *Playing Through*. New York: HarperCollins, 1998.

Chapter 1
Berra, Yogi. *The Yogi Book*. New York: Workman Publishing, 1999.
Covey, Stephen R. *Everyday Greatness*. Nashville: Rutledge Hill Press, 2006.
Reeve, Christopher. *Nothing Is Impossible: Reflections on a New Life*. Audio book. New York:
    Simon & Schuster, 2002.

Chapter 3
Armstrong, Lance, and Sally Jenkins. *It's Not about the Bike*. New York: Penguin Group
    Publishing, 2001.
Bascomb, Neal. *The Perfect Mile*. New York: Houghton Mifflin Company, 2004.
Canfield, Jack. *Success Principles*. New York: HarperCollins, 2005.

Chapter 4
Gwynn, Tony. *The Art of Hitting*. New York: GT Publishing, 1998.

Chapter 5
Dalton, Kathleen. "The Self-Made Man." *Time*, July 3, 2006, 56–57.

Chapter 6
Chungliang Al Hung, and Jerry Lynch. *Thinking Body: Dancing Mind*. New York: Bantam
    Books, 1992.
Dorfman, Harvey. *Coaching the Mental Game*. Lanham, MD: Taylor Trade, 2003.
Jackson, Phil. *Sacred Hoops: Spiritual Lessons of a Hardwood Warrior*. New York: Hyperion, 2001.
Mack, Gary. *Mind Gym*. New York: McGraw Hill, 2001.

Chapter 7
Robbins, Tony. *Unlimited Power*. New York: Simon & Schuster, 1997.
Rosenthal, R., and L. Jacobsen. *Pygmalion in the Classroom*. New York: Holt, Rinehart &
    Winston, 1968.
Steinberg, Gregg. *MentalRules for Golf*. Nashville: Towlehouse Publishing, 2003.

Chapter 8
Kriegle, Robert. *If It Ain't Broke, Break It*. New York: Warner Books, 1991.

Chapter 9
Goldberg, Alan. *Sport's Slump Busting*. Champaign, IL: Human Kinetics, 1998.
Maxwell, John. *Failing Forward*. Nashville: Thomas Nelson Publishers, 2000.

Chapter 10
Maltz, Maxwell. *The New Psycho-Cybernetics*. New York: Penguin Putnam, 2001.
Thomas, Marlo. *The Right Words at the Right Time*. New York: Atria Books, 2004.
Wade, Don. *And Then Justin Told Sergio*. New York: Contemporary Books, 1998.

Chapter 11
Ungerleider, Steven. *Quest for Success: Exploring the Inner Drive of Great Olympic Athletes.* Waco, TX: WRS Publishing, 1994.
Weinberg, Robert, and Dan Gould. *Foundations of Sport and Exercise Psychology.* Champaign, IL: Human Kinetics, 2004.
Woods, Tiger. *How I Play the Game.* New York: Warner Books, 2001.

Chapter 12
Coop, Richard. *Mind Over Golf.* New York: Simon & Schuster, 1993.
Dorfman, Harvey. *Coaching the Mental Game.* Lanham, MD: Taylor Trade, 2003.
Kriegle, Robert. *If It Ain't Broke, Break It.* New York: Warner Books, 1991.

Chapter 13
Loehr, James E. *Stress for Success.* New York: Three Rivers Press, 1997.

Chapter 14
Israel, Paul. *Edison: A Life of Invention.* New York: John Wiley, 1998.
Seligman, Martin. *Learned Optimism.* New York: Simon & Schuster, 1998.
Stolz, Paul. *Adversity Quotient.* New York: John Wiley, 1997.

Chapter 15
Loehr, James E. *The New Mental Toughness Training.* New York: Putnam Penguin, 1991.

Chapter 16
Feller, Bob, with Burton Rocks. *Bob Feller's Little Black Book of Baseball Wisdom.* New York: Contemporary Books, 2001.
McCallum, Jack. "The Rebounding Menace." *Sports Illustrated,* January 27, 1992, 54–56.

Chapter 17
Kriegle, Robert. *If It Ain't Broke, Break It.* New York: Warner Books, 1991.
Wegner, Daniel. "Ironic Processes of Mental Control." *Psychological Review* 101 (1994), 34–52.

Chapter 18
Lowe, Janet. *Michael Jordan Speaks.* New York: John Wiley, 1999.

Chapter 19
Martz, Maxwell. *The New Psycho-Cybernetics.* New York: Penguin Putnam, 2001.
Rotella, Bob, and Brad Faxon. *Putting out of Your Mind.* New York: Simon & Schuster, 2002.

Chapter 20
The Ultimate Athlete. Discovery Channel video, 1996.
Thomas, Marlo. *The Right Words at the Right Time.* New York: Atria Books, 2004.

Chapter 21
Ballesteros, Seve, and John Andrisani. *Seve Ballesteros: Natural Golf.* New York: Macmillan Publishing, 1988.
Gelb, Michael. *Discover Your Genius.* New York: HarperCollins, 2001.
Steinberg, Gregg. *MentalRules for Golf.* Nashville: Towlehouse Publishing, 2003.

Chapter 24
Kriegle, Robert. *If It Ain't Broke, Break It.* New York: Warner Books, 1991.
Naber, John. *Awaken the Olympian Within.* New York: Griffith Publishing, 1998.
Thomas, Marlo. *The Right Words at the Right Time.* New York: Atria Books, 2004.
Weinberg, Robert, and Dan Gould. *Foundations of Sport and Exercise Psychology.* Champaign, IL: Human Kinetics, 2004.

Chapter 25
Andrews, Andy. *Storms of Perfection.* Nashville: Lightning Crown Publishing, 1996.

Colvin, Geoffrey. "Twelve Peak Performers." *Fortune*, October 30, 2006, 104–122.
Dorfman, Harvey. *The Mental Game of Baseball*. South Bend, IN: Diamond Communications, 1989.
Gardner, Howard. *Extraordinary Minds*. New York: HarperCollins, 1997.
Schleier, Curt. "Leaders and Success." *Investors Business Daily*, August 13, 2004, A3.

Chapter 26
Hershiser, Orel, with Robert Wolgemuth. *Between the Lines: Nine Principles to Live By*. New York: Warner Books, 2001.
McEnroe, John. *You Cannot Be Serious*. New York: Penguin Group, 2003.

Chapter 27
Johnson, Michael. *Slaying the Dragon*. New York: Smithmark Publishers, 1997.

Chapter 28
Colvin, Geoffrey. "Twelve Peak Performers." *Fortune*, October 30, 2006, 104–122
Maltz, Maxwell. *The New Psycho-cybernetics*. New York: Penguin Putnam, 2001.
Steinberg, Gregg. *MentalRules for Golf*. Nashville: Towlehouse Publishing, 2003.
Thomas, Marlo. *The Right Words at the Right Time*. New York: Atria Books, 2004.

Chapter 29
Campbell, Joseph. *Pathways to Bliss*. Navato, CA: New World Library, 2004.
Greenberg, Jerold. *Comprehensive Stress Management*. New York: McGraw Hill, 2004.
Kriegel, Robert. *How to Succeed in Business without Working So Damn Hard*. New York: Warner Books, 2003.

Chapter 30
Alexander, Amy. "Writing Out of the Box." *Investors Business Daily*, October 20, 2004.
Coop, Richard. *Mind Over Golf*. New York: Simon & Schuster, 1993.

Chapter 31
Andrews, Andy. *Past Premiere Performances*. Audio CD collection. Lightning Crown Publishing, 2004.
Colvin, Geoffrey. "Twelve Peak Performers." *Fortune*, October 30, 2006, 104–122.
Williams, Pat. *How to Be Like Mike*. Deerfield Beach, FL: Health Communications Inc, 2001.

Chapter 32
Bradley, Bill. *Values of the Game*. New York: Broadway Books, 1998.
Greenberg, Jerold. *Comprehensive Stress Management*. New York: McGraw Hill, 2004.

Chapter 33
Bradley, Bill. *Values of the Game*. New York: Broadway Books, 1998.
Kelly, Matthew. *The Rhythm of Life*. New York: Fireside, 2004.
King, Larry. *My Dad and Me*. New York: Random House, 2006.
Lebell, Sharon. *Eptictetus: The Art of Living*. New York: HarperCollins, 1995.
Mack, Gary. *Mind Gym*. New York: McGraw Hill, 2001.
Schwarzenegger, Arnold. *Arnold: The Education of a Body Builder*. New York: Simon & Schuster, 1993.

Chapter 34
Gilbert, Brad. *Winning Ugly*. New York: Simon & Schuster, 1994.

Chapter 35
Maxwell, John. *Winning with People*. Nashville: Thomas Nelson, 2005.
Woods, Earl, and Fred Mitchell. *Playing Through*. New York: HarperCollins, 1998.

Chapter 36
Gelb, Michael. *Discover Your Genius*. New York: HarperCollins, 2002.

Romm, Ronald. Vanderbilt University. Personal communication, September 2006.
Ungerleider, Steven. *Quest for Success: Exploring the Inner Drive of Great Olympic Athletes.* Waco, TX: WRS Publishing, 1994.

Chapter 38
Insel, Paul, and Walton Roth. *Core Concepts in Health.* New York: McGraw Hill, 2002.
Kriegle, Robert. *If It Ain't Broke, Break It.* New York: Warner Books, 1991.
Loehr, James E. *Stress for Success.* New York: Three Rivers Press, 1997.

Chapter 39
Andrews, Andy. *The Traveler's Gift.* Nashville: Thomas Nelson, 2002.
Hamm, Mia. *Winners Never Quit!* New York: HarperCollins, 2006.

Chapter 40
Thomas, Marlo. *The Right Words at the Right Time.* New York: Atria Books, 2004.

Chapter 41
Bradley, Bill. *Values of the Game.* New York: Broadway Books, 1998.
Kriegle, Robert. *If It Ain't Broke, Break It.* New York: Warner Books, 1991.
Love, Davis, III. *Every Shot I Take.* New York: Simon & Schuster, 1997.

Chapter 42
Covey, Stephen. *Everyday Greatness.* Nashville: Rutledge Hill, 2006.
Steinberg, Gregg. "Pine Tar Nation." Tennessean.com, Oct 30, 2006.
Weinberg, Robert, and Dan Gould. *The Foundations of Sport and Exercise Psychology.* Champaign, IL: 2004.

Chapter 43
Carlson, Rolf. "The Socialization of Elite Tennis Players in Sweden." *Sociology of Sport Journal* 5 (1988), 241–256.
Gelb, Michael. *Discover Your Genius.* New York: HarperCollins, 2002.
Gregory, Andrew. Vanderbilt Sports Medicine. Personal communication, 2006.

Chapter 44
Kushner, Harold. *When Everything You Wanted Isn't Enough.* New York: Simon & Schuster, 1986.
Weinberg, Robert, and Dan Gould. *Foundations of Sport and Exercise Psychology.* Champaign, IL: Human Kinetics, 2004.

Chapter 45
Covey, Stephen. *Everyday Greatness.* Nashville: Rutledge Hill, 2006.
Horn, Thelma. *Advances in Sport Psychology.* Champaign, IL: Human Kinetics, 1994.
Player, Gary. *The Golfer's Guide to the Meaning of Life.* Emmaus, PA: Rodale, 2001.
Prabhu, Saritha, "Peace Prize Winner Yunus Exemplifies a Life Well-Spent." *Tennessean,* October 23, 2006.

Chapter 47
Parent, Joseph. *Zen Golf.* New York: Doubleday, 2002.

Chapter 48
Steinberg, Gregg. *MentalRules for Golf.* Nashville, TN: Towlehouse Publishing, 2003.

Chapter 49
Loehr, James E. *The New Toughness Training for Sports.* New York: Putnam Penguin, 1991.
Lynch, Jerry. *Creative Coaching.* Champaign, IL: Human Kinetics, 2001.
Seward, Brian. *Managing Stress.* Sudbury, MA: Jones & Bartlett, 2006.

Chapter 50
The Ultimate Athlete. Discovery Channel video, 1996.

ABOUT THE AUTHOR

GREGG STEINBERG, PhD, is an associate professor of sport psychology at Austin Peay State University. As a practitioner and internationally known speaker in this field, he is a frequent contributor to Fox News, CNN Headline News, and the Golf Channel. He is the author of *MentalRules for Golf* as well as the associate editor for the *Journal of Sport Behavior.* Dr. Steinberg is the head sport psychologist for the United States Golf Teacher Federation and has consulted with many college teams and professional athletes on the mental game. He lives in Nashville, Tennessee. If you would like to enroll in a Flying Lessons seminar or set up a mental game program for your child, please e-mail him at mentalrules24@msn.com, call (931) 206-1328, or visit his websites at corporatechampionconsulting.com and mentalrules.com.